Landscapes of
MALTA, GOZO
AND COMINO

a countryside guide
Seventh edition

Douglas Lockhart

SUNFLOWER BOOKS

Seventh edition © 2017
Sunflower Books™
PO Box 36160
London SW7 3WS, UK
www.sunflowerbooks.co.uk

ISBN 978-1-85691-503-8

Mdina Gate

Important note to the reader _____

We have tried to ensure that the descriptions and maps in this book are error-free at press date. The book will be updated, where necessary, whenever future printings permit. It will be very helpful for us to receive your comments (sent in care of the publishers, please) for the updating of future printings, and for the Update service described on the inside front cover of the book.

　　We also rely on those who use this book — especially walkers — to take along a good supply of common sense when they explore. Conditions change fairly rapidly on the Maltese islands, and **storm damage or bulldozing may make a route unsafe at any time.** If the route is not as we outline it here, and your way ahead is not secure, return to the point of departure. **Never attempt to complete a tour or walk under hazardous conditions!** Please read carefully the notes on pages 27 to 35, as well as the introductory comments at the beginning of each tour and walk (regarding road conditions, equipment, grade, distances and time, etc). Explore **safely**, while at the same time respecting the beauty of the countryside.

Cover photograph: Marsaxlokk (Car tour 2, Walks 20-21)
Title page: street name plaque (Vittoriosa, Walk 2)

Photographs: Douglas Lockhart, except for pages 26, 48-9, 107, 108, 118 and the cover: Shutterstock
Touring maps and town plans: Sunflower Books; walking maps adapted from maps produced by the Mapping Unit of the Malta Environment and Planning Authority, © Mapping Unit, Malta Environment and Planning Authority
A CIP catalogue record for this book is available from the British Library
Printed and bound in England: Short Run Press, Exeter

Contents

4 Landscapes of Malta, Gozo and Comino

☀ Preface

Malta, Gozo and Comino were visited by almost two million tourists in 2016, most of them from Britain, Italy, Germany and France. Many are there to enjoy typical Mediterranean weather; others see Malta as a change from the Spanish 'Costas', while a growing number are attracted by historic towns, museums and archaeological sites. Not everyone stays around the hotel pools or heads for the nearest beach and, during my visits, I have been pleasantly surprised to meet so many people like myself touring or walking in the countryside. The Maltese landscape offers rich rewards for those who enjoy exploring: interests in ancient and modern history, military and ecclesiastical architecture, geology, and flora are all well catered for. If this is your first visit to Malta, sampling a few of these walks will whet your appetite for many more return visits!

Landscapes of Malta, Gozo and Comino is divided into three main sections, each with its own introduction. **Motorists** will visit picturesque fishing villages, ancient ruins, high sea-cliffs, churches, and peaceful byways. **Picnickers** will be able to sample more than 30 lovely picnic spots, each of them surrounded by spectacular scenery or interesting man-made features. **Walkers** can enjoy gentle ambles or more strenuous hikes occupying a whole day; the walks visit the most exhilarating and spectacular landscapes on the three islands.

The history of the Maltese Islands dates back to Neolithic times, when settlers came from nearby Sicily, bringing with them domestic animals, agriculture and pottery. Since then the Phoenicians, Carthaginians, Romans, Arabs, Knights of St John, the French (for just two years), and the British have all left their marks of ownership. The islands are rich in prehistoric remains, among them the vast megalithic sanctuaries at Hagar Qim on Malta and Ggantija on Gozo, and tombs like the Hypogeum at Paola (Malta). More recent rulers, such as the Knights of St John, were responsible for building the impressive city of Valletta, and the defensive walls that guarded the city and its Grand Harbour against invaders are architectural masterpieces. The countryside is peppered with watchtowers and forts: some were built in

5

Victorian times; others, dating from World War II, reflect Malta's strategic position in the Mediterranean. The Maltese are a deeply religious people, and imposing churches and delightful chapels, many of which are open to the public, can be found everywhere. Valletta's National Museum of Archaeology, Palace of the Grand Masters of the Order of St John, and War Museum are well worth visiting.

Malta has been independent since 1964, becoming a republic ten years later. The last British forces left in 1979. Malta joined the European Union in 2004. The Republic consists of three main islands, Malta, Gozo and Comino, as well as a number of small uninhabited islets. Malta's land area is only 246 sq km (95 sq mi) and that of Gozo 67 sq km (26 sq mi), yet the Maltese Islands are home to a population of 420,000 — making them one of the most densely-populated areas in the world. Fortunately for lovers of the countryside, most Maltese live near Valletta and in a dozen other small towns, leaving much open countryside and unspoilt coast.

Over the centuries the Maltese people have come into contact with many nations and cultures that have tried to dominate them. As a result they are one of the most cosmopolitan of peoples. Paradoxically, the Maltese language has survived, although English is the co-official language and is spoken by almost 90% of the population.

Acknowledgements

Thanks to Sue Ashton for her contribution to the first two editions, and to the many 'Landscapers' who have made helpful comments.

Useful books

Frans A Attard, *The Maze: Comprehensive guide to streets of Malta & Gozo*, Uptrend Publishing, Birkirkara, 8th edition, 2016

Brian Blouet, *The Story of Malta*, Valletta, Progress Press, 8th edition, 2017

Leonard Mahoney, *5000 Years of Architecture in Malta*, Valletta Publishing, Valletta, 1996

Athanassios Migos (ed), *The Fortifications of Malta [by Quentin Hughes]*, Nearchos Publications, Rock Ferry, Wirral, 1997

Paul Murphy (ed), *Malta — Insight Guide*, Singapore, APA Publications, 5th edition, 2012

Geoffrey A Ross and Jonathan Beacon, *The Maltese Islands from the Air*, Proud Publishing, Balzan, 1994

Ray C Zammit (ed), *The Victoria Lines: Souvenir Guide*, Progress Press, Valletta, 1996

☀ Getting about

A **hired car** provides the means to explore Malta and Gozo at your own pace and can usually be hired at the larger hotels. International companies are represented in the main tourist centres and offer a range of modern cars. Local garages also have cars for hire, but these tend to be older. Rental prices are low and generally less expensive than UK rates.

Coach tours operate from hotels throughout the year and will take you to the major attractions on Malta and Gozo; they offer a useful introduction to history and scenery, but you won't get off the beaten track.

Public bus services are run by Malta Public Transport. A fleet of modern buses serve most places in Malta and Gozo on a regular basis. Each bus stop is named, announcements on the bus alert passengers to the next stop, and bus stops have timetables detailing services that call there. Buses on most routes run from early morning until late in the evening and provide an efficient way of travelling to the start of a walk and bringing you home at the end of the day. Ticket prices are inexpensive, and if you intend walking on most days of your stay, I recommend purchasing a 7-day ticket which allows unlimited travel on all services. Every walk in Malta and Gozo can be reached by bus, and there are frequent connections from the resorts to the bus terminus near City Gate in Valletta.

Bus services in Gozo have a basic hourly frequency, while the most direct service between the harbour at Mgarr and the main town of Victoria (Route 301) operates every half hour. I urge you to study Malta Public Transport's (hereafter MPT) very detailed website (public transport.com.mt) carefully — either before arriving in Malta or at your hotel. The site incorporates a 'journey planner' facility in which alternative routings and corresponding journey times are shown and provides timetables for all routes. It also has an update section detailing any service changes.

You should also obtain the **Malta Public Transport Route Map**, either by downloading a copy before you leave home or while in Malta from an MPT ticket office (at International Airport Arrivals or at the Valletta, Sliema

Ferry, Bugibba or Victoria bus station). In addition there are express services from the airport, services that call at the park and ride sites at Pembroke near St Julian's and Marsa, and night services at the weekend for those who might wish to combine night-life and walking.

Taxis operate from the major centres in Malta and, on Gozo, they are readily hired at Mgarr Harbour. Rates are controlled by the authorities and most taxi garages advertise fixed fares to popular destinations. Taxis are a comfortable and economical way of exploring routes not taken by coach tours, especially if the cost is shared.

Motorcycles and **bicycles** are an inexpensive way of getting around Gozo and can be hired in Victoria.

Inter-island ferries: The Malta–Gozo service is operated by roll-on/roll-off vehicle ferries belonging to the Gozo Channel Company, Channel House, Mgarr, Gozo (www.gozochannel.com). Weather permitting, a service between Marfa (opposite the Riviera Hotel), Cirkewwa (near the Gozo ferry terminal) and the Blue Lagoon in Comino is operated throughout the year by Comino Ferries Co-op Ltd (www.cominoferries.com). For telephone numbers and journey times on both services, see page 133.

Printed timetables are available for ferry crossings to Gozo and Comino (Comino Ferries Co-op Ltd). On pages 131-133 you will find bus timetables and ferry information covering the services used for the walks and picnics in this book, as well as services connecting the resorts with Valletta. Note that on **Malta** there are differences in service frequencies depending on day of the week and, in some cases, the season; space restrictions do not allow us to print all timetable variations. The heading 'Last bus' applies to Monday to Friday services. **Gozo** buses keep to the same timetable each day of the week. Please do not rely *solely* on the timetables in this book; check details of ferry sailings (especially if visiting Comino) and obtain the latest bus information from the MPT website, staff at one of the termini or by careful scrutiny of the timetable(s) displayed at every bus stop. A missed connection could spoil your day.

Bus departure points are shown on the town plans for Valletta (page 38), Rabat (page 44) and Victoria on Gozo (with the Gozo touring map inside the back cover).

Blue Lagoon, Comino (Picnic 27)

✱ Picnicking

Picnicking on the Maltese Islands is very much an informal activity, as there are relatively few locations, such as belvederes, with benches. However, the islands abound in spectacular settings on cliff-tops and delightful little coves where a private picnic can be enjoyed.

The following five pages contain all the information you need to get to more than 30 lovely picnic places. *Picnic numbers correspond to walk numbers,* so that you can quickly find the general location on the islands by looking at the touring maps (on which the area of each walk is outlined in white).

Many of these picnic spots are very easily accessible by bus, car or taxi and require only a short walk. Some, however, are best suited to those of you out for a ramble (for instance Picnics 7b, 21b, and 26d). I include walking times, transport details (🚌: how to get there by bus; 🚗: where to park), a map reference, and information about the views or setting. The location of the picnic spot is shown on the corresponding *walking map* by the symbol *P*. Several of the picnic places are illustrated.

Please remember that when one of the picnic suggestions is off the beaten track, you will want to wear sensible shoes and take a sunhat (○ indicates a picnic in full sun). It's a good idea to take along a plastic sheet as well, in case the ground is damp or prickly.

If you are travelling to your picnic by public transport, use the MPT website (see page 7) to verify the timetables on pages 131-133. You may be able to obtain similar information from MPT staff if your journey begins at one of the major centres (Valletta, Sliema Ferry or Bugibba on Malta; Victoria on Gozo). If your outward and return journeys use the same service, your driver may know the timetable for later in the day. *Always* check return ferry times on your outward trip, particularly if you need a bus connection at Cirkewwa.

If you are travelling by car, be extra vigilant off the main roads: farmers and their animals, and children in village streets may be unaware of traffic. Park well off the road, without damaging plants or blocking a road or track.

All picnickers should remember to read the Country code on page 34 and go quietly in the countryside.

4a Malta: Mellieha Bay (map pages 46-47) ○

by car or bus: up to 5min on foot
🚗 Park on the esplanade at Mellieha Bay; 🚌 41, 42, 49, 221, 222, X1 to Ghadira Police Station
One of Malta's best beaches. No shade, but there are several bars and restaurants nearby.

4b Malta: Marfa Ridge (map pages 46-47) 🎋

by car: up to 5min on foot
by bus: 40min on foot
🚗 Park at one of the picnic sites along the ridge road; 🚌 41, 42, 221, 222: alight at the roundabout (Qammieh bus stop) near the Red Tower and follow the ridge road eastwards (see Short walk 4-2 on page 47).
One of Malta's few organised picnic sites (signposted). Tables under the trees; shade. Views to St Paul's Islands.

4c Malta: Armier Bay (map pages 46-47, photo page 48) ○

by car: up to 5min on foot
by bus: 5-40min on foot
🚗 Park at Armier Bay (the third turn left off the Marfa Ridge road); 🚌 as Picnic 4b (with a 40min walk to the beach; 🚌 49 (summer only) to Armier Bay
Plenty of parking at this pleasant sandy beach, and a few bars and restaurants. A popular spot with the Maltese on Sundays and in the summer holidays.

5 Malta: Red Tower (map pages 46-47) ○

by car : up to 5min on foot
by bus: 5-10min on foot
🚗 Park off the side of the road near the tower, on Marfa Ridge; 🚌 as Picnic 4b, then follow Walk 5 on page 50.
Fine views of Mellieha to the south and Gozo to the north. Note: it can be very windy here!

6 Malta: Golden Bay (map page 54) ○

by car: 5-10min on foot
by bus: 5-10min on foot
🚗 Park near the Golden Sands Hotel; 🚌 44, 101, 223, 225 to Ghajn Tuffieha terminus; use

the map on page 54 to get to the beach.
Good sandy beach. No shade.

7a Malta: Triq Selmun (map pages 58-59) ○

by car: no walking
by bus: 10min on foot
🚗 Park at Selmun hamlet;
🚌 41, 42, 221, 222, XI: alight at Mellieha bus stop (near the roundabout on the outskirts of Mellieha), then follow the access road towards Selmun hamlet and the hotel.
A belvedere with seats and a fine view to St Paul's Bay.

7b Malta: Mgiebah Bay (map pages 58-59, photo page 12) ○

by car: 20-25min on foot
by bus: 40min on foot
🚗 Park near Selmun Palace;
🚌 as Picnic 7a above. Follow the start of Walk 7 (page 56) to reach the beach.
This is a peaceful little cove flanked by rocky headlands.

7c Malta: Mistra Bay (map pages 58-59) ○

by car: up to 5min on foot
by bus: 15-20min on foot
🚗 Park at Mistra Bay; 🚌 as Picnic 7a above: alight at Mistra bus stop; use the map on pages 58-59) to reach the beach.
A sheltered bay: good sunbathing, swimming and picnicking.

10a Malta: Victoria Lines (map pages 64-65, photo page 69) ○

by car: up to 5min on foot
by bus: 15min on foot
🚗 Park at the Lines: Take the Gharghur road (1km south of Bahar ic-Caghaq). Drive past the chapel shown on pages 66-67 and Villa Suzie (both on your left), then turn right on a narrow road to the Lines; 🚌 46: alight in Gharghur village. Follow the

road towards Madliena, then turn left on a road just 30m/yds before Villa Suzie.
Magnificent views; popular at weekends with the local people.

10b Malta: Victoria Lines Garden (map pages 64-65) ○

by car: up to 15min on foot
by bus: 25min on foot
🚗 and 🚌 as Picnic 10a. Follow notes for Picnic 10a, but continue 10 minutes more, to reach another small garden with seats.
Good views of the north coast.

11a Malta: Bingemma Gap (map pages 74-75, photo page 69) ○

by car: up to 5min on foot
by bus: 5min on foot
🚗 Park by the chapel at Bingemma Gap, northwest of Rabat;
🚌 51, 52 or 53 to Rabat interchange and 🚌 109 from there to Santi bus stop.
Picnic by the chapel; wonderful views over all of northern Malta.

11b Malta: Lippija Tower (map pages 70-71) ○

by car: 10-15min on foot
by bus: 25min on foot
🚗 Park off the side of the track to the tower (the track runs northwest from the Gnejna Bay road); 🚌 44, 101, 238: alight in Mgarr and follow Short walk 11-2 (page 69).
Magnificent seascapes, but keep away from the edge of the cliff!

12a Malta: Mtarfa, Belvedere on Triq Sir Philip Pullicino (map page 83)

by car: no walking
by bus: 3min on foot
🚗 Park at the belvedere; 🚌 51: alight at Castelletti bus stop (at the junction of Triq L-Imtarfa and Triq il-Konti F T Castelletti), then follow the latter until you can turn left at its junction with

Triq Sir Philip Pullicino.
Seats partly shaded by canopy, fine views of the Qlejgha Valley.

12b Malta: Gnejna Bay (map pages 74-75) ○

by car: up to 5min on foot
by bus: 40min on foot
🚗 Park at Gnejna Bay; 🚌 44, 101, 238: alight in Mgarr village and follow the road to the bay.
A pleasant bay, guarded by spectacular cliffs.

13 Malta: Public Garden at Targa Gap (map pages 78-79)

by car or bus: up to 5min on foot
🚗 Park on the track from the Victoria Lines; 🚌 31, 41, 42, 45, 48: alight at Targa Gap (Gharusa bus stop).
Public gardens on the outskirts of Mosta with good views of the countryside and St Paul's Bay.

15 Malta: Rabat (Tal-Virtu) (map pages 88-89) ○

by car or taxi: no walking
by bus: 5min on foot
🚗 Park at the viewpoint: on entering Rabat (from Valletta/Zebbug), drive along Triq Nikol Saura and Triq Gorg Borg Olivier, turn left on Triq Tal-

Virtu, and park 400m along, on the left; 🚌 51, 52: stay on the bus at the Rabat interchange and alight at the junction of Triq Tal-Virtu and Triq Gorg Borg Olivier (Ferris bus stop). Follow the blue signpost 'Seminarju' at this junction, to reach the viewpoint.
Seats at this viewpoint, opposite the Apostolic Nunciature, with wonderful views of the surrounding countryside to Mosta and as far as Valletta.

16 Malta: Buskett Gardens (map pages 88-89, photo page 92)

by car: up to 5min on foot
by bus: 5-10min on foot
🚗 Park at the Buskett Gardens; 🚌 56, 181 to Buskett.
Picnic anywhere in the unusual gardens. Shade of pines, citrus and a host of other trees. A popular spot at weekends.

17a Malta: Ghar Lapsi (map pages 94-95)

by car: up to 5min on foot
by bus: 20min on foot
🚗 Park at Ghar Lapsi; 🚌 201 to Bajjada bus stop, then walk to Ghar Lapsi
A very sheltered spot in windy weather; interesting fishermen's boats and jetties. Some shade at the huddle of boat-houses.

17b Malta: Wied Iz-Zurrieq (map pages 94-95)

by car: up to 5min on foot
by bus: 5min on foot
🚗 Park in the car park at the entrance to this village; 🚌 201: alight at the car park (Grotto bus stop) or 🚌 74: alight at the main road (Panorama bus stop). It's a stiff climb back up!
A spectacular steep-sided valley provides the backdrop, and the

Mgiebah Valley (Picnic 7a)

Salt pans at Blata l-Bajda (Walk 7)

fishing boats ferrying passengers to the Blue Grotto are a constant source of interest. Some shade at nearby village bars.

21a Malta: Gardens, St Thomas Bay (map page 105) ○

by car: 2min on foot
by bus: no walking
🚗 Park close to the gardens;
🚌 91, 119: alight at Bajja bus stop just before the San Tomaso bar on Triq Il-Qalet.
Pleasant terraced gardens overlooking the bay. Nearby bars and restaurants (some seasonal). Small sandy beach. Very popular at weekends.

21b Malta: Il-Qala-t-Tawwalija (map page 105) ○

only by car: 5-10min on foot
🚗 Park at the Ta' Kalanca car park at Delimara Point: this bar/restaurant is closed; *leave nothing of value in your car.* Then see the map on page 105. *A small sheltered cove.*

22 Malta: Blata l-Bajda (map page 109) ○

by car: 1min on foot
by bus: 5min on foot
🚗 Park on the seafront (Dawret ix-Xatt); 🚌 94, 120, 121: alight on the seafront (Penza bus stop).
Salt pans and a small bar which is popular with the local people.

23a Gozo: Belvedere on Triq Saghtrija, Zebbug (map pages 112-113) ○

by car: no walking
by bus: 10min on foot
🚗 Park just off Triq Saghtrija;
🚌 309: alight at Zebbug church
Superb views of Gozo's remote northwest coast from a hilltop viewpoint on the edge of the village. Seats. No shade.

23b Gozo: Xwieni Bay (map pages 112-113, photo page 113) ○

by car: up to 5min on foot
by bus: 5-10min on foot
🚗 Park at Xwieni Bay.
🚌 310 to Xwienji bus stop, then on foot
Picturesque cove with salt pans and dramatic cliffs.

24a Gozo: Xlendi (map pages 116-117)

by car: up to 5min on foot
by bus: 5min on foot
🚗 Park in Xlendi village; 🚌 306, 330 to Xlendi.
There are any number of water's-edge picnic spots on the way to Xlendi Tower. Some shade near the harbour bars and restaurants.

24b Gozo: Dwejra Bay (map pages 116-7, photo page 26) ○

by car: 5-10min on foot
by bus: 2min on foot
🚗 Park at Dwejra and refer to the notes on page 118.
🚌 311 to Dwejra
Wear sturdy shoes to explore the Inland Sea. Wonderful coastal scenery, diminished a little by the collapse during a storm of the Azure Window in

Cliffs overlooking Dahlet Qorrot

2017. The sea cliffs nearby are very dangerous, as signs warn. Dwejra Tower, open when the flag is flying, is worth visiting. Little shade except at the Inland Sea.

25 Gozo: Mgarr ix-Xini (map pages 120-121) ○

only by car: 2min on foot
🚗 Limited parking on the minor road from Xewkija, on the southwest side of the valley.
Fjord-like inlet; very sheltered; fishermen's boat houses; restaurant/bar.

26a Gozo: Hondoq ir-Rummien (map pages 124-125) ○

only by car: up to 5min on foot
🚗 Park at Hondoq ir-Rummien, southeast of Qala.
A water pipeline and a disused quarry nearby don't detract from this secluded little bay overlooking Comino.

26b Gozo: Dahlet Qorrot (map pages 124-125) ○

only by car: up to 5min on foot
🚗 Park at Dahlet Qorrot, northeast of Nadur.
There's pleasant picnicking near the boat houses, but no shade.

14

26c Gozo: Gnien San Blas, Nadur (map pages 124-125)

by car or bus: no walking
🚗 Park nearby; do not attempt to drive down the narrow road to San Blas Bay; 🚌 303: alight at Weraq bus stop where the bus turns before retracing its outward route back into Nadur.
A garden with seats, some shaded by a canopy, on the outskirts of the village, overlooking the San Blas Valley.

26d Gozo: San Blas Bay (map pages 124-125)

by car: 15-20min on foot
by bus: 15-20min on foot
🚗 Park on the northern outskirts of Nadur village; don't try to drive down the steep narrow road, as turning is very difficult; 🚌 as Picnic 26c above.
Delightfully secluded. Shade by the boat houses.

27 Comino: Blue Lagoon (map page 129, photo page 9) ○

by boat: up to 5min on foot
⛴ See page 128 for details.
Picnic on the rocks. No shade.

☀ *Touring*

Car hire in the Maltese Islands is inexpensive and when this book was first published in 1989 was a way of getting to some of the more isolated areas. The very significant improvements to bus services in Malta and Gozo, coupled with the ever-increasing volume of road traffic and parking difficulties in the towns have much reduced the advantage of car travel compared with public transport. Although **driving is on the left-hand side of the road**, it can be a tiring experience, especially in the hot sun.

The main roads have received considerable investment in recent years, and pavements and cycle lanes have been added when roads have been rebuilt. However, in the towns, hazards such as double parking, building sites, construction vehicles parked at the roadside, drivers illegally using mobile phones, potholes and complicated junctions abound, so keeping alert is absolutely vital.

Many **secondary roads** have been upgraded to allow buses to use them, but others wind between stone walls and afford only restricted views. Some remain poorly surfaced and suffer from limited maintenance. The touring map shows all the roads I would recommend for motoring, but you may find it interesting to refer to the large-scale *walking maps* while touring, because of their wealth of detail.

The touring notes are brief: they include little history or information available in standard guides or tourist office literature. I concentrate instead on 'logistics': distances, road conditions, the finest viewpoints, and clear directions as to the best route (where signposts might let you down). Above all, the touring notes emphasise possibilities for **walking** and **picnicking**. The symbol *P* alerts you to a picnic spot; see pages 9-14. While some of the suggestions for walks and picnics may not be suitable during a car tour, you may find a landscape that you would like to explore at leisure another day.

The fold-out touring map is designed to be held out opposite the touring notes and contains all the information you will need outside the towns. **Town plans** are included for Valletta (page 38), the Three Cities (page 40), Rabat/Mdina (page 44) and Victoria on Gozo (with the Gozo touring map inside the back cover).

Both of the tours on Malta start and finish in the main resort area of Sliema; the Gozo tour begins at Mgarr harbour. However any of the tours can be joined from other points without difficulty.

Symbols used in the touring notes correspond to those on the touring map; see map key for explanation.

Some points worth noting

- Before setting off, check that the car has a jack and spare tyre.
- **Speed limits** are as follows: 35 kmph in built-up areas, but occasionally 25 or 30 kmph; 50, 60 or 70 kmph elsewhere.
- Priority on **roundabouts** is given to traffic already negotiating the roundabout.
- In the event of an **accident**, removal of the car (even if it is blocking the traffic) before the arrival of the police will invalidate the insurance.
- **Allow plenty of time** for visits; the times given only allow for very brief stops at viewpoints.
- Public **WC**s are more widely available than in most European countries; others are found in bars.
- In towns only **park** your car where permitted.
- **Petrol stations** are open between 06.00 and 18.00. Automatic machines provide 'out of hours' service at many stations. A number of new petrol stations have been built in recent years.
- **All motorists should read the Country code on page 34 and go quietly in the countryside.**

Harbour at St Julian's (Car tour 1)

Car tour 1 MALTA: RESORTS, BEACHES, AND HISTORIC TOWNS

Sliema • Salina Bay • Mellieha • Cirkewwa • Golden Bay • Mgarr • Bingemma Gap • Rabat • Mdina • Mosta • Naxxar • San Gwann • Sliema

71km/44mi; about 2h30min driving
On route: Picnics (**P** symbol; see pages 9-14): 4a, (4b, 4c, 5), 6, (7a), 7b, 7c, (10a, 10b), 11a, (11b), 12a, 12b, (13), 15; Walks 3-15

A leisurely tour on asphalted roads of variable quality, with some superb views and coastal scenery. The western ridge and coast roads tend to be narrow and steep, requiring especially careful driving.

This drive visits the northern and western parts of the island and includes two contrasting coastlines — one low and rocky, attracting much tourism development, and the other bounded by high perpendicular cliffs with few access points to the sea. The second half of the tour passes through the interior, where the rural landscape features a succession of ridges and valleys before arriving at the historic walled town of Mdina. From there it is only a short journey back to the waterfront at Sliema.

Head northwest out of Sliema on the coast road to **St Julian's★** (2.7km 🏖🍴🛒), a fast-developing resort area boasting many five-star hotels. Just up from the bay, fork left (following signposting for St Andrew's) and then turn right on the main road at the top of the rise (signposted to St Andrew's, St Paul's Bay, Mellieha). You are now on the dual carriageway coast road and heading for quieter countryside. This road has recently been

rebuilt — welcome news, as the old road contained many tricky bends and was reputed to be one of Malta's most dangerous roads.

Just past the old Pembroke Barracks, a road on your left leads up to Gharghur (**P**10a, 10b). Continue straight on to **Bahar ic-Caghaq**. Walk 10 ends here, having descended from the Victoria Lines. Continue on around to **Ghallis Point** and Tower (10.5km 🏛), setting for

Walk 9. Fishing from the rocks, as well as the marine park, provide attractions in this coastal area which slopes gently to the sea. **Salina Bay**, with its salt pans, is the next port of call. The rash of modern development at Bugibba appears on the skyline. (It is possible to divert into Bugibba, Malta's response to the Spanish 'Costas', by turning off right and then bearing right again to Qawra Point. From there continue on through Bugibba, rejoining the road at St Paul's Bay.)

Ignore the bypass and go through the town of **St Paul's Bay** (San Pawl il-Bahar; 14.5km ▲▲✕🗗), to enjoy the local colour. The small harbour is worth a visit — it's a piece of old Malta, tucked away from the new development. Carry on through **Xemxija**, where Walks 7 and 8 end. A small road on the left (signposted Mistra) takes us under the main road and down to **Mistra Bay** (18.5km ☞**P**7b). The road winds through a gentle agricultural landscape to a secluded bay.

Return to the main road, which winds its way through several hairpin bends up to the village of **Mellieha** (22km ♦✕🗗☞ and access to **P**7a). There are several new hotels and restaurants in the main street and many characterful local shops. Just past the large reddish-coloured church, there is a fine viewpoint. The road descends to **Ghadira** and **Mellieha Bay★** (23.5km ▲▲✕

The beautiful old Casa del Tesoriere in pristine Mdina's Pjazza Tas-Sur

*P*4a), a very popular sandy beach. Walk 6 starts here, and Walk 5 ends here. The Ghadira Nature Reserve is off to the left.

Drive up to the next ridge now, via more hairpin bends. From here diversions (not included in the mileage) may be made to the left (to the Red Tower; *P*5) or to the right, to Armier Bay (*P*4c; photograph page 48) or the Madonna statue at the end of Marfa Ridge (☂*P*4b). To reach Armier Bay take the third turning left off the ridge road, near a shrine. The main road continues to the Gozo ferry harbour at **Cirkewwa** (32km 🚢), but you can visit Paradise Bay by branching off left just before the hotel of the same name.

Retrace your route from Cirkewwa to the roundabout at Ghadira (36km, just below the Mellieha Ridge. For a different perspective, take the bypass this time and, towards the top of the ridge, at the roundabout on the outskirts of Mellieha village, turn right (signposted Ghajn Tuffieha). This narrow road winds through ridge and valley country (past the track to the Ghajn Snuber Tower) to the agricultural village of **Manikata** (40km). Then it descends to the crescent-shaped sandy beach of **Golden Bay★** (🚢✕ *P*6b), where Walks 6 and 11 end.

From Golden Bay turn right towards the next bay (Ghajn Tuffieha), left at a T-junction, and then right again onto the

Ta' Saliba/Zebbieh road. At Ta' Saliba turn right for **Mgarr** (45km ♨🚻) and its distinctive domed church, shown on page 20. In the village centre, turn right and descend to **Gnejna Bay** (47.5km *P*12), where you'll see colourful boat houses and dramatic rock formations. Walk 12 nears its end here.

From the bay return to Mgarr. Under 2km uphill you pass the turn-off left to the Lippija Tower (*P*11b), one of the settings for Walk 11. Drive straight through Mgarr and take a road on the right on the outskirts of the village. This steep narrow road takes you through the imposing Dwejra Lines at **Bingemma Gap** (53km 📷), the starting point for Walk 11 and about halfway along the route of Walk 13 (photograph page 69). The views from the little chapel (*P*11a) are wonderful and well worth a stop. Descend from the ridge, crossing over the head of the Chadwick Lakes (Walk 13) and making for Rabat.

Arriving at the **Busugrilla round-about*** opposite the Nigred housing estate (starting point for Walks 12 and 14), continue to historic **Mdina★** (57km ♨M🚢 ✕📷). Parking is available near the Roman Villa. The 'silent city' of Mdina, into which traffic is restricted, is one of Malta's most beautiful places. Walk 3 ambles round Mdina and its suburb, **Rabat** (♨✕🚻), where there are catacombs and more imposing buildings. Walk 15 begins at Tal-Virtu, in the southeastern

---

*I highly recommend a detour from the Busugrilla roundabout to the remote western coast: follow the signs for Fiddien Bridge. The road runs parallel with the *wied* initially and eventually descends to the foot of

high vertical cliffs via a series of hairpin bends. The spectacular scenery is exhilarating. Allow 13km return (not included in the mileage) and beware: some maps do not show this road system correctly.

Mosta Dome and (left) inside the church, decorated for Christmas

corner of Rabat (**P**15).
Leaving Mdina, descend the hill and follow the signs to **Mosta★** (61km ♣✖️🍴⊕), the starting point for Walk 13. Mosta's enormous domed church (said to be the fourth largest unsupported rotunda in the world) is your next target. Short walk 8 and Walk 13 end at Targa Gap on the outskirts of town, where there are public gardens offering fine views of St Paul's Bay (**P**13).

From Mosta Dome fight your way through the traffic, following the road signs for St Paul's Bay, to a roundabout on the outskirts of the town. Follow signposts to Naxxar at both this roundabout and the next one. Turn right into **Naxxar** at 64.5km, passing the residence of the British High Commissioner. Under 2km along, turn left at a roundabout (signposted to San Gwann/Sliema). Driving through this conurbation is always difficult. On the outskirts of **San Gwann** (67.5km), which is a Maltese 'new town', turn right for Gzira/Msida, ignoring the road straight ahead, signposted for Sliema. (The road straight ahead *would* get you back, but it is a more complicated route.) Continue to follow the Msida/Gzira signs into the fashionable area of Kappara, until you reach a roundabout on the Sliema regional road. If you carry straight on here, you will come to the Gzira seafront and then turn left for Sliema (71km).

Car tour 2 MALTA: ANTIQUITIES, FISHING VILLAGES AND GARDENS

Sliema • Hypogeum • Marsascala • Marsaxlokk • Wied iz-Zurrieq • Hagar Qim • Ghar Lapsi • Buskett Gardens • San Anton Gardens • Sliema

74km/46mi; about 2h30min driving
On route: Picnics (**P** symbol; see pages 9-14): 16, 17a, 17b; Walks 14, 16-22. (Picnics 21a,

21b and 22 are not far off the touring route.)
A comprehensive tour on roads of reasonable quality, with varied and interesting scenery.

T his drive complements Tour 1 and shows you the rest of Malta. Pretty fishing villages, fascinating ancient monuments, historic gardens, and the Blue Grotto combine to make this a really memorable drive.

From Sliema hug the interesting little creeks southwards to **Pietà** (4km), passing the yacht marina at Ta' Xbiex. Continue by looping underneath the Floriana/Marsa road, then head uphill to join it. Follow signs for Marsa and, on approaching an industrial estate, signs for Paola (⊕). You skirt the shipyard near high-density housing estates. The **Hypogeum** (8km 🏛) is signposted: the vast underground tombs and temple are well worth a visit. The nearby Neolithic temples at Tarxien (less than a kilometre from the Hypogeum) are also highly recommended. Your ongoing route follows signposting for Fgura and Zabbar; a mosque provides a landmark, indicating that you are on the correct road. Pass the Hompesch Arch (11.5km) and, on the outskirts of Zabbar, turn right for the picturesque fishing village of Marsascala (signposted). **Marsascala★** (15km 🏛🏖✕🍽) is an ideal spot to recuperate from all the heavy traffic and indulge in a fish lunch at one of the many waterfront cafés. Walk 21 starts out here; Walk 22 begins and ends here. Take heart, the roads are relatively quiet from now on. Turn left along the promenade towards the former

Jerma Palace Hotel and St Thomas Tower. After passing the hotel, turn right, then left, on the road leading down to St Thomas Bay, where there are more restaurants (✕**P**21a). Turn right to **Zejtun** (19.5km 🏛), a typical and unspoilt large Maltese village with an impressive late 17th-century church, worth seeing for its richly-painted interior. The route through this village is also complicated: after passing the bus terminus on the eastern outskirts, bear right at the first church, skirt around the main church in the centre, and then follow signs for Tarxien — to escape Zejtun from the west. Eventually you should come to the main Valletta/Birzebbuga road. Turn left here towards Birzebbuga, then turn left again, driving through vineyards to **Marsaxlokk★** (24km 🏛✕🍽), the attractive village shown on pages 102-103. Walk 20 begins here, and Walk 21 ends here.

Take the coastal road out of Marsaxlokk to St George's Bay, passing the Ferretti Battery. On reaching the main road, turn right for the archaeological site and museum of **Ghar Dalam** (🏛; under 1km return) or go straight across to the fortified

Bronze Age village of **Borg in-Nadur**★ (27.5km 🏛). The latter is visited on Walk 20.

Keep to the coastal road via **Birzebugga** into **Pretty Bay**, which unfortunately has now acquired an industrial backdrop. Head towards Kalafrana but, at 30km, follow the main road around to the right, towards the old Hal Far airfield (now an industrial estate). Just beyond the airfield turn left for Zurrieq, a small town which poses yet more navigational problems: at about 36km, on the outskirts, turn left (opposite St Agata Church) into the centre of **Zurrieq**. The main church is reached in under a kilometre (37km ⚔🏪). Continue straight on (circling the church) to the bypass. Turn left on reaching the bypass and follow signs for Wied iz-Zurrieq/Blue Grotto. The road provides some spectacular views on the descent to **Wied iz-Zurrieq**★ (40km ⚔📷 **P**17b), and the little inlet is an exciting picnicking spot. Walk 17 ends here.

Retrace your route uphill and, in about a kilometre, turn left for the prehistoric temples of **Hagar**

The silver domes of Dingli church (left) and view northwest along the Dingli Cliffs (above)

Qim and **Mnajdra** (🏛) — famous for their lovely setting close to the sea, from where they look out to the off-shore island of Filfa (a nature reserve). The road continues west to a roundabout; turn left here to the picturesque hamlet sheltering in a bay under the cliffs, **Ghar Lapsi** (46.5km ✕📷*P*17a) — a delightful picnicking and swimming spot visited on Walk 17.

Return to the roundabout and go straight over this time, following signs to the outskirts of **Siggiewi** (♻🚻; Walks 18 and 19). The agro-tourism 'Limestone Heritage' attraction★ on the village outskirts is interesting. Bear left around this town, following signposting for Rabat, and turn off left at a crossroads (where a poorly-surfaced road from Zebbug comes in from the right). This roughly-surfaced road leads up the Girgenti Valley, twice crossing the route of Walk 16, and emerges at the impressive vertical Dingli Cliffs (see Walk 14 and photograph on page 84). Turn right past the army post to **Dingli** (58km ♻✕),

with its distinctive silver-domed church, visible from miles around.

A signposted road on your right, in the centre of the village, leads you to **Verdala Palace** (60km ◨✕; photograph page 92) and the **Buskett Gardens** (*P*16), further settings for Walk 16. The palace, which was once the summer residence of the Grand Masters and is now a government guesthouse for VIPs, is only open very occasionally to visitors, but the gardens are open daily.

From Verdala Palace make for Rabat and then follow signs for Attard and Valletta. The **Ta' Qali Craft Village** and the **National Park★** (signposted on the left) are worth visiting on weekdays. At 67.5km turn off left (signposted Balzan/San Anton) to the **San Anton Gardens** and the President's imposing residence, for a shady stop amongst subtropical plants (Walk 4).

The final stage of the tour reenters the conurbation and goes through **Birkirkara** and **Msida** to Sliema (74km).

Car tour 3 GOZO: A HIDDEN GEM

Mgarr • Ir-Ramla • Marsalforn • Victoria • Dwejra Bay • Xlendi • Mgarr

40km/25mi; about 1h45min driving

On route: Picnics (*P* symbol; see pages 9-14): 24a, 24b, 26e; Walks 23-26. (Picnics 23a, 23b, 25 and 26a-c are not far off the touring route.)

A gentle little tour on roads of variable, but generally good quality; this circuit includes most of Gozo's highlights.

A visit to Gozo is usually regarded as the highlight of a holiday in the Maltese Islands. It is less urbanised, and its greater dependence on agricultural activities make it ideal for touring. The landscape is characterised by flat-topped hills that seem to rise out of terraced fields, and a dozen or so small villages each dominated by a honey-coloured church.

The tour starts and ends at Mgarr, on the assumption that most visitors will come over on the ferry from Malta. (Walks 25 and 26 also start here). On arrival at pretty **Mgarr** harbour (✕🍴), it is better to let the crowds disperse rather than join the convoy of vehicles up the hill. Taking some leisurely refreshment at one of the quaint waterside bars allows one to appreciate the picturesque little harbour.

Climb uphill on the main road and, at the first bend, turn right towards Qala and Nadur on a narrower road which hugs the cliff-edge. Under one kilometre from the harbour, turn right along Triq Zewwieqa. On reaching the outskirts of **Qala** (2.5km) there is a good viewpoint (📷 with seats) looking out over Comino and northern Malta. Almost immediately, turn left towards the village centre, then turn right on reaching the main road and go left at the *pjazza* and parish church, in the direction of Nadur. (Alternatively, go straight ahead and make a short detour towards the eastern suburbs, to view a large windmill that is unfortunately not open to the public.) Climb steadily, then bear left at the top of the street into more modern housing, much of it built by returning emigrants who have spent their working lives in Australia, Canada or the USA. Head for the neighbouring village of **Nadur**, which enjoys commanding views from its ridge-top position. Like Qala, Nadur is a typical Gozitan community, with its large church, central square with a few shops and bars, and much new suburban housing.

From Nadur just follow signs to beautiful **Ir-Ramla★** (7.5km 🏛; photograph page 33), a large golden sandy beach visited on Walk 26. Retrace your route from the bay for only a few hundred metres and then branch off on a minor road on the right. At first it follows a watercourse in the Ramla Valley, and in under another kilometre it swings right and then left, climbing towards the southern edge of the sprawling hilltop village of **Xaghra** (10.5km ▲✕✝🏛📷). Turn right at the T-junction (but

Mgarr harbour, where the car tour and Walks 25 and 26 begin

bear left if you wish to visit the impressive prehistoric temples of Ggantija, only a few minutes away, in a fenced enclosure; **∏**) and then proceed more or less straight through Xaghra to **Marsalforn** (13km 🚤✕🚩📷), an old fishing town which is now a popular resort. Take the main road up the valley to **Victoria**, the capital (🚤✕🚩♁⊕📷**M**), which is well worth exploring. Walks 23 and 24 radiate from Victoria, and Walk 25 ends here.

On reaching the main street in the centre of Victoria (Triq ir-Repubblika) turn right, passing the citadel on higher ground on the right; then follow signs for San Lawrenz and Dwejra. At just over 19km a detour of about 3km may be taken, to the isolated church of Ta' Pinu (♁), famous for its miracles: take the road on the right towards Ghammar. The quaint little village of Gharb (Walk 23) is also worth a visit on this diversion; it has an attractive

church, a folk museum, and a timeless village square. When you regain the main road, turn right to San Lawrenz.

At **San Lawrenz** the road forks left to **Dwejra Bay** (***P***24b) and the **Inland Sea★** (22.5km 📷). The descent to Gozo's most remote corner is quite barren and spectacular. Here you will find magnificent vertical cliffs, Fungus Rock (see overleaf), and a large, shallow enclosed pool which is perfect for swimming. This is one of the settings for Walk 24.

The only realistic way to get back to Victoria is to retrace your outward route. On reaching the outskirts of Victoria (just past the isolated Gelmus Hill on the left), fork right (signposted Kercem/Santa Lucija) and follow the signs to Xlendi, passing the Knights' wash-house★. The road winds its way down a narrow ravine to the little fishing village at the bottom. **Xlendi★** (31.5km 🚤✕ 📷***P***24a), with its pastel-coloured houses sheltering at the end of a fjord, is one of the most picturesque places in the Maltese Islands. It is also a very popular lunch venue with tourists. Some two-storey housing on the waterfront has been replaced by taller buildings, as can be seen in the photograph on page 115. The bay is still delightful for swimming, and if you fancy a picnic, you can find quiet seats on the esplanade that leads towards Xlendi Tower. Walk 24 passes through here.

Return to Victoria and, this time, turn right at Pjazza San Frangisk for the return ferry from Mgarr. Xewkija Dome, which may be larger than Mosta Dome, is the most striking feature of the return trip. For another good viewpoint over the harbour, turn right by the church along Triq Lourdes, just before the final descent to the quayside in Mgarr (40km).

Fungus Rock, one of Gozo's landmarks, is all that remains of the rock wall which once enclosed Dwejra Bay (Picnic 24b)

☀ Walking

The Maltese Islands may appear small compared with other Mediterranean islands. A glance at a map also suggests that Malta is densely populated; however you'll be surprised and delighted to find varied scenery and many hidden places in the countryside. Gozo, with its slower pace of life, is a walkers' paradise — a richly cultivated landscape overlooked by hilltop villages. The cliff scenery on both Malta and Gozo is breathtaking, while tiny Comino offers tranquillity and some fine views.

The walks in this book are intended as day excursions that are accessible by public transport and should give you an excellent cross-section of land- and seascapes on all three islands. Obviously there are many other walking possibilities, but access by public transport might be a problem. If you have a car at your disposal, you can use the maps to create your own walk combinations.

There are walks in this book for everyone.

Beginners can start on the walks graded 'easy': be sure to check all the short and alternative walks — some are easy versions of the longer hikes. You need look no further than the picnic suggestions on pages 9 to 14, to find a large selection of gentle strolls, many on level ground. The town walks are fairly short and, apart from some steps in Walks 1 and 2, are on flat ground. Otherwise, I particularly recommend Walks 4, 5, 18 and 22.

Experienced walkers: If you are accustomed to rough terrain you should be able to enjoy all the walks in this book. But note that a couple of the hikes demand a head for heights. Take into account the season and weather conditions, too. Don't attempt the more strenuous walks in high summer. Always remember that heavy rainfall could make any walk described in this book unsafe! If you have not come to one of the landmarks after a reasonable time, please go back to the last sure point and start again.

Experts: There are few walks to challenge you, so relax and enjoy the exhilarating scenery and fascinating history.

Waymarking, maps, GPS

Signposting of walks has only recently begun on the islands. Tracks and footpaths abound in areas that are intensively cultivated, but many peter out in fields.

Walk 12: view downstream over the Chadwick Lakes, from the bridge crossed 10 minutes into the walk

The routes described in this book have been overprinted on 1:25,000 **maps** published in 2009/2010 by the Planning Authority in Floriana. (To save space, we have reduced the maps to a scale of 1:32,000.) These maps, divided into two sheets, are **GPS compatible:** UTM (33S) projection, Datum European 1950. But the handiest and most economical one-sheet map is Kompass map 235 Malta/Gozo at a scale of 1:25,000. Those of you who work with GPS will be pleased to know that **GPS tracks for all the walks are available for free download** from the Malta/Gozo page on the Sunflower website.

Walkers' checklist

The following points cannot be stressed too often:

- **Never walk alone.** Four is the best walking group: if someone is injured, two people can seek help, so there will be no need to panic in an emergency.
- **Do not overestimate your energies.** Your speed will be determined by the slowest walker in your group.
- **If a walk becomes unsafe**, do not try to press ahead.
- **Transport connections** at the end of a walk are very important.
- **Proper shoes** or boots are vital.
- Always take a **sunhat** with you, and in summer a cover-up for your arms and legs as well.
- **Warm clothing** is needed on the ridges and coasts, especially in windy weather and after sundown. Even in summer, take it along, in case you are delayed.
- Carry **water and food** with you, especially on the longer walks.
- **Compass, whistle, torch, first-aid kit and mobile phone** weigh little, but could save your life.
- A **stout stick** (or your walking pole) is a help on rough terrain and to discourage the rare unfriendly dog.
- Read and re-read the **Important note** on page 2 and the **Country code** on page 34, as well as guidelines on grade and equipment for each walk you plan to do.

What to take

If you are already on Malta when you find this book, and you do not have items like a rucksack, you can still enjoy a number of the easier walks, or you can buy some equipment in one of the sports shops. Please do not attempt the longer or more difficult walks without the proper equipment. For each walk described, the absolute *minimum* equipment is given. Do modify the equipment according to the season: for instance, carry a long-sleeved shirt and long trousers as well as a sunhat in summer, and put them on before noon to avoid sunburn; take cardigans and raingear on cooler days. Above all, you need thick-soled stout shoes or walking boots which provide good ankle support. The often stony and dusty tracks on the islands can be unforgiving towards the improperly-shod walker.

Please bear in mind that I have not done *all* the walks in this book under *all* weather conditions. I may not realise just how hot or how wet a walk can be in certain seasons. Be particularly vigilant when there is a cool breeze: you can still get sunburn or sunstroke.

If you intend going to Malta properly kitted-out, you may find the following checklist useful:

stout shoes or walking boots (broken-in and comfortable)	small/medium-sized rucksack knives and openers
long trousers, tight at the ankles	lightweight jacket
waterproof clothing (outside summer months)	whistle, compass string, clips, safety pins
first-aid kit (bandages, plasters etc)	walking pole(s) extra bootlaces
torch (if only for inspecting the darkened interiors of small chapels…)	plastic rainhat plastic cups, plates 2 light cardigans
long-sleeved shirt (for sun protection)	extra pairs of socks plastic groundsheet
'Dog Dazer' (see page 32)	sunhat, sun cream
up-to-date bus and ferry timetables (see pages 7-8)	telephone numbers of taxi operators

I rely on your good judgement to modify our equipment according to circumstances and the season.

Weather

The climate is typically Mediterranean, with long hot summer days and mild winters. **Rainfall** is mainly confined to the months of September to April and, even then, there are relatively few days when the sun does not shine. Strong **winds** are a feature of the climate: these help to moderate the high summer temperatures, but bear in mind that they add to the chill factor in winter, especially if you are walking on the ridges or the cliffs. Always carry warm clothing with you in the winter months; wind chill is always a possible risk in exposed locations.

The **best months for walking** are February to May, when the countryside is a riot of wild flowers and the crisp northwesterly winds ensure superb visibility. October and November are good months too. *If you walk in winter*, note that after heavy rain some of the crossings over normally-dry *wieds* (valleys) may be difficult.

AVERAGE TEMPERATURES AND RAINFALL

month	average air temperature				average sea temperature		average hours of sun	average rainfall in
	minimum		maximum					
	°C	°F	°C	°F	°C	°F		mm
Jan	9.5	49	15.0	59	14.5	58	5.3	88.2
Feb	9.4	49	15.4	60	14.5	58	6.3	61.4
Mar	10.2	50	16.7	62	14.5	58	7.3	44.0
Apr	11.8	53	18.7	65.5	16.1	61	8.3	27.5
May	14.9	59	23.0	73.5	18.4	65	10.0	9.7
Jun	18.6	65.5	27.4	81.5	21.1	70	11.2	3.4
Jul	21.0	70	30.2	86.5	24.5	76	12.1	0.9
Aug	21.8	71	30.6	87	25.6	78	11.3	9.3
Sep	20.2	68.5	27.7	82	25.0	77	8.9	44.4
Oct	17.1	63	23.7	75.5	22.2	72	7.3	117.9
Nov	13.8	57	19.9	68	19.5	67	6.3	75.5
Dec	11.1	52	16.7	62	16.7	62	5.2	96.0

Photography

Photography is forbidden in military areas, but you will encounter few Armed Forces posts on the walks.

Where to stay

If your chief interest is a walking holiday on Malta, it would be best to stay in the north, particularly **Mellieha** or **Bugibba**. You will have a wide choice of walks nearby, and the Gozo ferry is within easy reach. There is also interesting walking near **Rabat** in the west. However, most accommodation is in the **Sliema/St Julian's** area — a little far from some walks, but with excellent buses.

For a really relaxing time, away from the pace of modern life, try **Gozo**: the good ferry service means that visits to northern Malta are well within reach, while Comino is just a stone's throw away. An ideal contrast would be to spend a week in Bugibba and another tucked away on Gozo.

The Malta Tourism Authority publishes an accommodation list which includes hotels, tourist villages, aparthotels, guest houses and hostels.

Maltese pronunciation and place names

In Malta, the co-official languages are Maltese and English. English is spoken by approximately 90% of the population. Italian, French and German are also quite widely understood. But since accession to the European Union, the newly formed National Council for the Maltese Language is encouraging greater awareness of the local language. One result is the greater use of Maltese place names rather than their English counterparts. This can be seen on the MPT website, for example, where the destination of BUS 1 from Valletta is shown as Isla (Senglea). *This book uses the more familiar English place names,* but the index includes their Maltese equivalents — for example Cospicua (Bormla).

Obviously it is not necessary to know any Maltese when asking directions or buying bus tickets, but it *is* helpful to be able to pronounce place names.

Maltese alphabet and vowel sounds

Ħħ	The double barred H is hard, the nearest English equivalent being h as in *house*, but in Maltese it is very strongly aspirated, thus Mellie-**ħa** (Mellieħa).
GĦ, għ	is silent: **Ine**-sielem (Għajnsielem)
Ċċ, Ġġ, Żż	A dot over these consonants indicates a softening in pronunciation, thus **Ch**-irkewwa (Ċirkewwa).
Jj	is pronounced as y.
Qq	is silent, but may be pronounced as k in rural dialects.
Xx	sounds like sh, thus **Sh**-lendi (Xlendi).
Aa	is pronounced as a in fast.
Ee	is pronounced as e in wet.
Ii	is pronounced as ee in eel.
Oo	is pronounced as o in dock.
Uu	is pronounced as oo in loot.
Aj	is pronounced as i in ice.

Some place-name elements

Aħrax	rugged	**Marsa**	harbour, inlet
Baħar	sea, bay	**Misraħ**	wide-open space
Bir	well	**Nadur**	look-out point
Blata	rock	**Qala**	bay, inlet
Borġ	tower	**Qortin**	promontory
Ġebel	rocky hill	**Pjazza**	square
Għajn	spring	**Ramla**	sandy beach
Għar	cave	**Ras**	headland
Ġnien	orchard, garden	**Rdum**	cliff
Ħal	village	**Triq/trieq**	street/road
Kbir	large, great	**Wied**	valley
		Xagħra	rocky plateau

Prefixes to place names

il-, iċ-, id-, in-, ir-, is-, it-, ix-, iż- *the*
ta' *of*
taċ-, tad-, tal-, tan-, tar-, tas-, tat-, tax-, taż- *of the*

Examples:
Għajn Tuffieħa *the spring of the apples*
Wied il-Busbies *valley of fennel*
Għar Dalam *the cave of darkness*
Ġnien tal-Isqof *the little garden near the bishop's vale*

NB: With the exception of street names, Maltese spellings are not used in the text, lest they slow up your reading, but they *are* used on the *walking* maps and in the index beginning on page 134.

Nuisances and hazards

Be aware that **shooters** and **trappers** are about, particularly at weekends and holidays (see box opposite). Cliff-tops and much of the open countryside are reserved for bird-shooting. Some hunters don't seem to mind walkers disturbing them; inevitably there are exceptions. *All hides are best approached with caution and passed by quickly and quietly.*

Most **dogs** are chained, but I mention the (very few) places where they might be a problem. Information about ultrasonic 'Dog Dazers' can be obtained from Sunflower Books, who sell them.

Although you could encounter fairly large black **snakes** on Gozo and Comino, they are not poisonous.

Throughout the Maltese Islands there are many old military buildings and watchtowers. While these add interest to the walks in this book and can be useful landmarks for walkers, some small **gun emplacements** are hazardous and are best not entered. Larger structures, such as forts which are not yet open to the public, should not be explored.

Malta, Gozo and Comino have extensive areas of high cliffs, as well as some rocky under-cliff areas. **Keep a safe distance from the cliff-edge and avoid all cliff areas in periods of windy weather**. Paths that are close to cliff-edges, erosion, loose surfaces and strong winds are hazards that can combine to make parts of the Delimara Peninsula in Malta and extensive coastal areas in Gozo extremely dangerous. Although you may see other walkers heading towards these areas, I strongly recommend that the following paths *(which are **not** used in this guide)* should be avoided: each contains at least one stretch that I believe is unsafe.

— the coastal path after 1h17min along Il-Hofra z-Zghira (Walk 21)

— from Wied il-Mielah west towards Il-Ponta ta'Hekka (Walk 23)

— the coastal path from Wardija Point to Dwejra (Walk 24)

Prickly pear leaves are used as little individual wind-breaks to protect young seedlings in the San Blas Valley.

Shooting and trapping

If you have not visited the Maltese Islands before, be warned that when you are out walking, you may be distressed by the **shooting and trapping of birds** — a controversial tradition which does little to endear the islands to visitors.

Letters are often written to the Ministry of Tourism, and several have also appeared in the European press, commenting on the slaughter of so many migratory birds.

Yet this activity is perfectly legal and, indeed, has long historical roots. The Knights, for example, deliberately planted trees to create environments in which the shooting of birds took place. Today this pastime is carried on by several thousand Maltese men, usually in cliff-top areas and in the more hilly parts of Malta and Gozo.

Some hunters and bird-trappers do not go out of their way to object to the presence of walkers in the vicinity. Others are much less comfortable about sharing the countryside with people who are simply there to enjoy the scenery, and evidence of this can be seen in the various 'keep out' and 'private' signs, as well as gates, fences and various other barriers that have mushroomed in some parts of Malta in recent years.

There are two kinds of activity which you will notice at some points on almost all the walks. Firstly, **small shooting hides** which are best passed by quickly and quietly. Sometimes you will also see small cages on rock pillars, containing decoy sparrows and chaffinches. Secondly, hides are sometimes associated with areas of ground that have been cleared of loose stones and on which **nets and wires** have been laid to trap birds. These devices are quite small-scale (measuring no more than 15-20m/yds by 4-5m/yds and are mainly found in cliff-top areas.

If shooting is taking place close by, *additional caution is required,* and it is best not to look skywards just in case spent cartridge shot is falling. It is worth wearing *sunglasses* if you do find yourself in an area where shooting is occurring. *Bright-coloured clothing* will also make your presence visible to shooters. Avoid colours such as green, brown and grey, as these blend into the landscape too easily.

— the path beyond the western end of the paved section of the Sanap Cliffs scenic walkway in the direction of Xlendi Tower (Walk 24)

— the cliff-top section east of the defensive wall (25min-point) to Il-Gebel tah-Hawla (Walk 26)

— the 'short-cut' through the Mistra Rocks between Dahlet Qorrot and San Blas Bay (Walk 26)

— In addition, after wet weather the descent on the clay slopes beyond Fort Campbell (Walk 7) can be very slippery and walking poles are required.

Country code for walkers and motorists

The experienced rambler is accustomed to following a 'country code' on his walks, but the tourist out for a lark can unwittingly cause damage, harm animals and even endanger his/her own life. A code of behaviour is important wherever people are free to roam over the countryside, and doubly so on rugged terrain. On the Maltese islands, special care should be taken to avoid fires.

- **Do not light fires** or allow children to play with matches. Never throw cigarette ends away in woodland. If you see a fire in or near woodland, telephone to inform the police.
- **Do not frighten animals.** By making loud noises or trying to touch or photograph them, you may cause them to run in fear and be hurt.
- **Do not leave gates open**, unless that is how you find them. Although animals may not be in evidence, the gates do have a purpose; generally they keep grazing or herded sheep or goats in (or out of) an area.
- **Do not pick wild or cultivated plants.** Leave them in place for others to enjoy. Flowers would die before you got them back to your hotel, and fruit is obviously someone's livelihood.
- **Do not pollute the countryside with your litter.**
- **Do not block roads or tracks** when driving. Park where you will not inconvenience anyone or cause danger.
- **Do not take risks while out walking.** Don't attempt walks beyond your capacity. Remember that there is very little twilight on Malta. If you were to injure yourself, it might be a very long time before you were found. Do *not* walk alone, and *always* tell someone responsible — perhaps at the hotel desk — exactly where you are going and what time you plan to return. On any but a very short walk near villages, be sure to carry a first-aid kit, whistle, torch, an extra woolly and plenty of water. It's a good idea to take along some high-energy food like chocolate, too.

Organisation of the walks

Each of the 27 rambles in this book was chosen for its accessibility from the main tourist resorts. They fall into six groups: town walks, northern Malta around Mellieha and Bugibba; western Malta, centred on Rabat, Dingli and Siggiewi; southeastern Malta, with Marsaxlokk and Marsascala as the focal points; Gozo; and Comino. The small size of the islands and the efficient public bus system will ensure that there are several walks near your resort, and many others only a short trip away.

The book is set out so that the walks can be planned easily. You might begin by looking at the touring map inside the back cover. Here you can see at a glance the overall terrain, the road network, and the orientation of the individual walking maps in the text. Quickly flipping through the text, you'll also find that there's at least one photograph for each walk.

Having selected one or two potential excursions from the map and photographs, look over the planning information at the beginning of each walk: distance/time, grade, equipment and how to get there. There are almost always short and alternative versions of the main walk; if even these seem like too much effort, turn to the picnic suggestions for gentle after-lunch strolls. Alternatively, the energetic can use the notes and maps to combine the walks and make long hikes.

When you are on your walk, you will find that the text begins with an introduction to the overall landscape and then quickly turns to a detailed description of the route itself. The **maps** (all reproduced at a scale of 1:32,000) show key landmarks. **Times** are given for reaching many of these landmarks. Timing depends on many factors but, once you've done one walk, you'll be able to compare my times with your own pace. Note that the times given *do not include any stops!* Allow extra time for picnics, photography and the like.

Below is a **key to the symbols** on the walking maps:

▬▬▬	trunk road	🚌 🚏	bus stop.best views
▬▬	other main road	Ch.Cha.Sch	church.chapel.school
▬▬	local road	Hosp.Pol Sta	hospital.police station
══	minor access road, lane	Bks.Cem	barracks.cemetery
══════	tunnel	✚ 𝔗ower	antiquity (tower, palace, etc)
------	track/footpath	▪ Resr ○	water tank.reservoir.spring
2 →	walking route and direction	✇ □	quarry.specific building
2 →	alternative route	P 🚗	picnic spot and nearby car
—40—	height (in metres)		parking (see pages 9-14)

Walk 1 MALTA: VALLETTA — CAPITAL AND PLANNED TOWN

Distance: 3.7km/2.3mi; about 1h
Grade: quite easy, but there is a steepish ascent from the War Museum back to the centre, and another on the optional detour to Victoria Gate.

Equipment: comfortable walking shoes, sunhat
How to get there and return: 🚐 to City Gate (Valletta bus terminus).

Valletta was planned as a fortified town shortly after the Turks withdrew following their unsuccessful Great Siege of Malta in 1565. The town occupies much of the Sciberras Peninsula, on ground that is higher than the Three Cities (Walk 2) which lie on the south side of the Grand Harbour. Laid out on a grid plan designed by the Italian architect Francesco Laparelli, Valletta was named after the Grand Master of the Knights of St John, Jean de La Vallette. Impressive fortifications, fine public buildings and the legacy of strict planning regulations are among the features which make this walk memorable. But unfortunately, streets laid out in the 16th century are not ideal for vehicle access to business premises: while much of the main shopping street (Triq Ir-Repubblika) has been pedestrianised, on some of the other narrow streets your progress will be impeded by vehicles parked on the pavements.

To **start out**, enter the **City Gate**, the scene of recent redevelopment. You will immediately pass the open air theatre on the site of the Royal Opera House, destroyed in a bombing raid during World War II. Take the first right just beyond the building site (Triq Nofs-in-Nhar) and you will arrive at Castille Place, overlooked by the beautiful **Auberge de Castille et Leon**, now the Prime Minister's office. Continue straight ahead (the old Garrison Church, which has been converted into the Stock Exchange, is on your right) and enter the **Upper Barracca Gardens**, where the stunning views of the Grand Harbour, the Three Cities and the dockyard must be among the most photographed scenes in Malta. Walk back to the entrance of the gardens and turn right into Triq Sant' Ursula. In 60m/yds turn right again, then almost immediately left into Triq Il-Batterija. Just beyond the British Hotel there is a small café with tables in the open air overlooking the Victoria Gate, the quayside entrance to the city. In this area you have a first look at the very tall tenement houses, many with distinctive balconies, and the clever way in which streets and steps have been planned to accommodate the steeply-sloping ground. Pause for a moment at the FOOTBRIDGE OVER Triq Il-Lvant or, better still, take a 15-minute detour down some steps, to see the beautifully-restored Victoria Gate and the wharves near the old fish market.

Resuming the main walk, St Barbara Bastion with its shady trees overlooking the harbour gives way to Triq Mediterran and more pleasant greenery, the **Lower Barracca Gardens**, where there is a kiosk. From here the walk turns northeast, passing the **Mediterranean Conference Centre** (formerly the Sacra Infermeria of the Knights of St John) and **Fort St Elmo**, the scene of heroic resistance against the Turkish forces during the Great Siege. Just beyond the main fort entrance is the **National War Museum**, containing relics of the battle for Malta during World War II. The next building of interest is the **Auberge de Bavière**, the former residence of the Bavarian Knights, which now houses the Government Property Department. The vistas along this stretch are towards Sliema and the old forts and barracks on Manoel Island and Tigne, which has been transformed by new buildings.

The bastions, seen from the old fish market

VALLETTA

i	Tourist Information	8	War Museum	17	Triton Fountain
1	City Gate	9	Auberge de Bavière	18	The Malta Experience
2	Auberge de Castille	10	Auberge d'Aragón	19	Archbishop's Palace
3	Upper Barracca Gardens	11	St Paul's	20	Theatre
4	Victoria Gate	12	Grandmaster's Palace	21	Fine Arts Museum
5	Lower Barracca Gardens	13	Armoury	22	Law Courts
6	Mediterranean Confer-	14	National Library	23	Ferry to Three Cities
	ence Centre	15	St John's (also Museum)	24	Bus Terminus
7	Fort St Elmo	16	Archaeological Museum	25	Old Fish Market

Pass the **House of Catalunya** (Ministry of European Affairs) and immediately turn left up some steps (Triq L-Arcisqof), to reach a small square (Pjazza Independenza), with the **Auberge d'Aragón** on your left. Then turn right into Triq Il-Punent (where **St Paul's Anglican Pro-Cathedral** is on your right). Take the next left (Triq Il-Tiatru) to reach the main squares in the heart of the city. On the south side of Pjazza San Gorg is the **Grandmaster's Palace** — worth visiting to see the state rooms decorated with 38

magnificent paintings depicting the Great Siege, and the **Armoury**. Proceed west along Triq Ir-Repubblika, past Misrah Ir-Repubblika, a square with several good cafés. It is over-looked by the **Malta National Library** which contains the archives of the Knights. You are now entering the main shopping area; **St John's Co-Cathedral** is off to the left and the **National Museum of Archaeology** is further along on the right. A few minutes walking should see you back at **City Gate**.

Walk 2 MALTA: THE THREE CITIES: COSPICUA, SENGLEA AND VITTORIOSA

Distance: 6.4km/4mi; about 1h25min
Grade: easy, with only a few flights of steps. Little shade on the bastions, some shade in Vittoriosa
Equipment: comfortable walking shoes, sunhat, water
How to get there and return: 🚌 2, 4 from Valletta to/from Riche bus stop (Vittoriosa).

Departures every 10min; journey time 20min. Or 🚌 124 from Marsascala; departures hourly; journey time 25min.
Short walk: Cospicua — Senglea (3.2km/2mi; 40min; easy). Shorten the walk by returning from the main square in Senglea (Misrah Papa Benedittu XV); take 🚌 1 from Redentur bus stop to Valletta.

A dockyard, an industrial estate on the horizon and some of Malta's (indeed the world's) highest urban population densities may seem a less than ideal backdrop for a walk. And the bus journey from Valletta, passing an apparently-endless succession of industrial sites, gives few clues to the unique character of the communities of Cospicua, Senglea and Vittoriosa on the south bank of the Grand Harbour. But these areas are ideal for strolls in late afternoon (winter) or early evening (summer), when the low sun highlights the dramatic mix of architecture: housing, public buildings, churches and ramparts.

The **best place to start** is the VITTORIOSA BUS TERMINUS. Walk towards the head of **Dockyard Creek** and the centre of **Cospicua**, passing the quayside known as XATT IR-RISQ. The former dockyard is on your right; here, in the 16th century, the Knights of St John repaired their galleys. For almost 150 years this was the site of the No 1 Dock of the Naval Dockyard; it has been transformed into leisure use, the area around has been landscaped, and a new footbridge links Cospicua and Senglea. The footpath passes local bars, the band club, the church and shops. Some five minutes along, turn right and climb slightly uphill to TRIQ SAN PAWL, where the Suez Canal Bar is on your left.
Another five minutes sees you at the WALLS OF **Senglea**: proceed straight through the arches into the main square (MISRAH PAPA BENEDITTU XV). On the left is the impressive parish church, **Our Lady of Victories**. The original 18th-century church was destroyed during World War II; the present building, with a war memorial in front, dates from the 1950s. Like other waterfront communities in Malta, Senglea suffered a great deal from bombing raids aimed at ships berthed in the adjacent creeks and the dockyard.
Just beyond the church, turn left on TRIQ SAN LAWRENZ, which leads to TRIQ IS-SUR and the western bastions of Senglea. Here you'll see supertankers and other large vessels in the main dockyard. Continue along Triq-is-Sur as far as the junction with TRIQ SAN FILIPPU, then turn right. In two minutes you come to the late 17th-century church of **St Philip Neri**, overlooking a small square (PJAZZA FRANCESCO ZAHRA PITTUR 1710-1773). Pass

COSPICUA SENGLEA VITTORIOSA

N 0 300 m / 300 yds

Vittoriosa

Kalkara Creek

Kalkara

Santa Scolastica
La Valette
San Filippu
Il-Palazz l'Antik
San Anton
11 Port of England
12 Mandragg
E.A Bezzina
Misrah ir-Rebha 1565
Hilda Tabone
Triq il-Mina l-Kbira

San Lawrenz

Xatt il-Forn

Senglea

Triq Is-Serena

Triq iz-Zewg Mini

Dockyard Creek

French Creek

Triq is-Sur

Triq San Lawrenz

Misrah Papa Benedittu XV

Triq San Lawrenz

Xatt ir-Risq

Il-Gublew

Cospicua (Bormla)

Triq San Pawl

1 Bus Terminus (Vittoriosa)
2 Our Lady of Victories
3 St Philip Neri
4 Macina Bastion
5 St Lawrence Church and Freedom Monument
6 Maritime Museum
7 Fort St Angelo
8 Gate of Provence and Post of France
9 Inquisitor's Palace
10 Ferry to Valletta
11 Port of England
12 Port de Allemagne

the church and turn left on TRIQ IZ-ZEWG MINI; this leads to a small GARDEN at the tip of the peninsula, with fine views of Valletta, Fort St Angelo in Vittoriosa and the entrance to the Grand Harbour. The small sentry box, known locally as a *gardjola*, is worth inspecting — including the inscriptions that are a reminder of less secure times, when maritime communities needed to be vigilant against invaders and pirates.

Leaving the gardens, bear left down one flight of steps (the second flight leads to a small playing field) and turn right along TRIQ IS-SERENA — a fine example of a small back street. Turn left to the quayside, where

there are several open-air bars. To end the Short walk, turn right into TRIQ SAN LAWRENZ and return to the main square (**40min**).

The main walk continues along the quayside; passing under the arch in the huge bastion known as the **Macina**, continue to the footbridge, cross it, and turn left. Almost immediately you pass the landing point of the passenger ferry to Valletta and walk straight ahead to **Vittoriosa**'s parish church of **St Lawrence**. This was an important place of worship for the Knights of St John. The present church dates from the 17th century and is worth visiting. There are many impressive paintings in its chapels and another, behind the

Senglea's church, Our Lady of Victories, from French Creek

altar, of the town's patron saint. In front of the church is the **Freedom Monument**, built in 1979 to commemorate the embarkation of the last British military forces on HMS London. Every year, on 31 March, there are ceremonies and a regatta to mark this event.

Continue beside the quay, XATT IL-FORN, to the **Maritime Museum** (open daily), housed in the former Naval Bakery. The next landmark is the old Scamp Palace, which has been converted into the Casino de Venezia, and an apartment complex (St Angelo Mansions Block 1) has recently been constructed further along the quayside. Moorings have been built, and the Grand Harbour Marina is already attracting yachts. Two minutes past the museum, go straight ahead over the BRIDGE and walk about 50m/yds along the waterfront (XATT SANT ANGLU), to a point opposite the the ramp up to **Fort St Angelo (1h)**. At the tip of the Vittoriosa promontory, this fort played a major role in repulsing repeated attacks of the Turkish Armada during the Great Siege of 1565. More recently, it was the Mediterranean headquarters of the British fleet.

The fort is not open to visitors. Retrace your steps to the St Angelo Mansions (**1h02min**) and turn left up a flight of steel steps between it and the adjacent building. Reach a street and turn left, then go right in 30m/yds and take another flight of steps past a small electricity sub-station. You reach the end of TRIQ IL-HABS L-ANTIK. There was once a high-level access to Fort St Angelo at this point, but it has been severed as part of the redevelopment of the waterfront. Walk along the street for some 100m/yds, then turn left onto the eastern bastions of Vittoriosa which overlook **Kalkara Creek**. The route is along TRIQ EMANUEL ATTARD BEZINA and TRIQ IL-MANDRAGG. After climbing two short flights of broad steps, leave the walls by turning right into a small square (**1h10min**).

At the right-hand corner of the square, by a house named Ave Maria, take a very narrow street (TRIQ IL-FOS). In only a few yards/metres you come to a junction where there is a small shop. Turn right into TRIQ HILDA TABONE. Follow it, then turn left into TRIQ IT-TRAMUNTANA and pass the 13th-century **Norman House** on your left before turning right into TRIQ IL-MAJJISTRAL, where the main attraction is the huge **Auberge d'Angleterre.** Turn left to regain TRIQ HILDA TABONE near the **Auberge de France** and reach Vittoriosa's main square (MISRAH IR-REBHA; **1h17min**). Although most of the buildings that overlook the square are modern — due in part to the heavy bombing of this area during World War II — they are still interesting. The Band Club

41

Top: Grand Harbour marina from Xatt il-Forn, Vittoriosa; bottom: Dry Docks complex from Senglea (left), Freedom Monument and St Lawrence Church in Vittoriosa (right)

boasts a green balcony, the Labour Party Club has some traditional Maltese balconied windows currently in maroon livery, while the Sala Parrokkaji resembles administrative buildings found in eastern European cities.

The exit from the square is the street furthest to the left (TRIQ IL-MINA L-KBIRA). In two minutes you come to the restored

fortifications of the **Gate of Provence**, on your right. There are superb views of Senglea from the **Post of France** high on the walls, and the complex also houses the Malta at War Museum.

Retrace your steps back to the street, turn right and find the BUS TERMINUS for Valletta just across the main road (**1h25min**).

42

Walk 3 MALTA: MDINA AND RABAT

See also photograph page 2
Distance: 3.2km/2mi; 45min-1h
Grade: an easy walk, with plenty of shade in summer
Equipment: comfortable walking shoes, sunhat
How to get there and return:
🚌 51, 52, 53 from Valletta to/from Rabat; alight at Pjazza Saqqajja (just after the bus climbs a steep hill). Return from the bus stop on the opposite side of Pjazza Saqqajja.
Short walk: Mdina
(1.4km/0.9mi; 25min). Follow the main walk to Mdina and, after completing the circuit of the town, return to the bus stop at Pjazza Saqqajja, Rabat.

Mdina is often called 'The Silent City' — something of a misnomer, since it is estimated that four out of every five tourists who come to Malta visit Mdina during their stay. Mdina received its name from the Saracens, who ruled Malta in the 9th century and strengthened the walls and ditches which separate Mdina from the suburb of Rabat. Although Christianity was restored to Malta by the Normans in the 11th century, the subsequent history of Mdina was characterised by neglect, culminating in the arrival of the Knights of St John who preferred to develop defensive settlements around the Grand Harbour. In contrast, Mdina became the home of most of the Maltese nobility, and it is their palaces and houses which give the city much of its appeal to today's visitors. Rabat, by contrast, tends to be overlooked by many tourists, which is a little surprising, as it contains the site where St Paul is said to have preached, as well as many interesting buildings.

The bus climbs a steep hill to enter Rabat. Alight from the bus at the first stop in the town: Saqqajja (the bus then continues to Rabat interchange). **Start out** by walking through PJAZZA SAQQAJJA and head for the **Gnien Howard** (gardens) and **Mdina Gate** (photograph page 2), reached in about five minutes. Cross the ditch and walk through the gate, to a small square. Now most visitors continue along the main street (TRIQ VILLEGAIGNON); I recommend a different, quieter route but, if you follow the crowds, it is a ten-minute walk past souvenir shops, cafés and St Paul's Cathedral to the Pjazza Tas-Sur, where you can pick up the main walk.

My walk heads between Mdina Gate and the bastions. Turn left into TRIQ INGUANEZ and follow it through PJAZZA TAL-MINA TAL-GRIEGI. Turn right into TRIQ L-IMHAZEN (Magazines Street) and almost immediately come to **Mina Gharreqin**, from where there are fine views of the countryside — and some architectural curiosities. The old British naval hospital at Mtarfa is on the horizon, and the former terminus (now a restaurant) of a narrow-gauge railway line to Valletta lies in the valley floor. From Mina Gharreqin take TRIQ L-IMHAZEN where, on the left, you will see a long warehouse building which was used to store armaments. Three minutes past

43

here, turn right into TRIQ IL-KARMNU, which leads to the northern end of TRIQ VILLEGAIGNON. Turn left here, to **Pjazza Tas-Sur**. From the bastions there are panoramic views of Mosta and St Paul's Bay and, on a clear day, it is possible to pick out Valletta's churches on the skyline.

To return to Mdina Gate, walk to the eastern end of Pjazza Tas-Sur, pass the Fontanella Tea Garden on your left and follow narrow TRIQ IS-SUR and then TRIQ SANTU ROKKU to **St Paul's Cathedral**, which was rebuilt after a massive earthquake in 1693. Nearby are the **Archbishop's Palace** and **Cathedral Museum**. From the square proceed through a second

St Paul's Cathedral. Like many churches on the island, Mdina's cathedral has two clocks. In this case, the second clock shows the day and month. But in most cases, the second clock has a painted, fixed time — to confuse the Devil.

square (PJAZZA TA L-ARCISQOF) to TRIQ SAN PAWL, passing the **St Benedict Convent** and **Palazzo Vilhena**, once the seat of the 'Universita' (office of local administration), now a natural history museum. When you arrive back at Mdina Gate, cross the ditch and turn right into Gnien Howard, where there are seats and some shade. Beyond the gardens is Rabat interchange and a car park, and at a road junction you come to the **Museum of Roman Antiquities** (often referred to as the 'Roman Villa'), where the mosaics of a Roman town house and other finds can be seen. The walk now crosses the road into TRIQ SAN PAWL. Narrow alleys and typical Maltese balconies now vie for your attention, and there are plenty of bars for refreshments.

Among the landmarks along Triq San Pawl are the L'Isle-Adam Band Club in the Palazzo Xara, which boasts a magnificent curved balcony, and the St Mary of Jesus Friary. Soon you come into PJAZZA PAROCCA, the focal point for streets in Rabat. The square is dominated by **St Paul's Church**; the open area beside it, where St Paul preached his sermons, is crowned by his statue. Pass the entrance to the church and bear left into TRIQ IL-KULLEGG. Plaques on the wall here commemorate the visits of Pope John Paul II in 1990 and of Pope Benedict XVI in 2010. Both Popes had visited Rabat to pray at St Paul's Grotto, where St Paul lived during his stay on the island. A well-signposted route along TRIQ SAN KATALDU and TRIQ SANT'AGATA leads to **St Paul's Catacombs and Museum**. Another historical complex, **St Agatha's Catacombs and Crypt**, is also only a few minutes walk from the PJAZZA PAROCCA.

Return to St Paul's Church and turn right through the pedestrian area, passing an octagonal obelisk commemorating the kindness shown by the Maltese people to St Paul, then turn sharp right into TRIQ COSMANA NAVARRA (or take the next right, Triq il-Kbira, if you prefer the hustle and bustle of Rabat's main shopping street). Triq Cosmana Navarra, a typical narrow street, leads to the **National Archives**.

Turn left at the junction and follow TRIQ L-ISPTAR past the Local Council Offices (at the junction with TRIQ IL-KBIRA). Continue straight on and in under a minute turn right into TRIQ SANTU WISTIN. Proceed through a little square (MISRAH SANTU WISTIN), and the bus stop at SAQQAJJA is straight ahead (**45min-1h**).

Walk 4 MALTA: GHADIRA • MADONNA STATUE • ARMIER BAY • MARFA

Distance: 10km/6.2mi; 2h30min

Grade: easy, with ascents/descents of 45m/150ft overall

Equipment: stout shoes, sunhat, swimwear, waterproofs, picnic, water

How to get there: 🚌 41, 42 from Valletta (every 30min, journey time about 1h); 🚌 222 from Sliema (every 30min, journey time about 50min); 🚌 221 from Bugibba (every 30min, journey time 25min). Alight at the entrance to the Mellieha Holiday Centre adjacent to the Ghadira police station.

To return: 🚌 41, 42 from Marfa to Valletta

Short walk 1: Ghadira — Madonna statue — Red Tower (6.4km/4mi; 1h40min; easy). Follow the main walk to the statue; return along the ridge road and catch 🚌 41, 42 from the roundabout near the Red Tower.

Short walk 2: Red Tower — Marfa (3.5km/2.2mi; 55min; easy). Take 🚌 41, 42 to the roundabout near the Red Tower and follow the ridge road east. Take either the second small road left to Ramla tal-Qortin or the third road left to Armier Bay.

This walk highlights the varied landscapes of the Marfa Ridge, where isolated bays and cliff scenery dominate. The area has also attracted some international hotel chains, and on the northern flanks there is a large concentration of Maltese holiday homes.

Leave the bus on the seaward side of the police station at **Ghadira** and **start out** by walking north along the sandy beach of **Mellieha Bay** (Picnic 4a). At the end of the beach pass in front of Sol Beach Restaurant and climb up to the access road leading to the MELLIEHA BAY RESORT HOTEL. After passing the entrance to hotel reception, reach a pole barrier to prevent vehicle access and walk to the far end of the car park. Take a path that in one minute descends steeply through abandoned terraces, and in two minutes meet the COASTAL PATH (**25min**). Turn left and follow this to **Ta' l-Imgharrqa**; a steep

path leads down to this almost enclosed, circular bay, but you continue high above it (**30min**).

Keep parallel with the FORTI-FICATIONS. The coastal path widens out into a clear track, and you come upon the ruins of a jetty; a RED AND WHITE CONCRETE PILLAR stands nearby. Continue on a footpath, making sure that you do not walk too close to the cliff edge; the rocks here are very unstable. After passing a pole barrier preventing vehicle access, merge with the ridge road (**50min**) and follow it to the right. Successful afforestation has resulted in both sides of the road becoming wooded, something of a rarity on Malta, and a chance to enjoy a picnic in the shade (Picnic 4b).

At **1h**, at the top of the hill, a wide panorama opens up, encompassing Comino and Gozo to the left and St Paul's statue just around the headland on the right. At **1h10min**, arrive at an OLD CHAPEL and MADONNA STATUE. Enjoy the fine views (while keeping away from the cliff-edge), with perhaps the added interest of a cruise ship or supertanker making for port. Retrace your steps along the ridge road for some 400m/yds, then take a track (TRIQ IX-XMAJJAR) on the right (**1h15min**) leading through walled fields flanked by prickly pear and pine trees. At **1h30min** the track reaches the coast at the MALTA CAMPSITE, where there is a bar. Turn left around the perimeter of the campsite on a track to

Ramla tat-Torri (Slug Bay; **1h40min**). (A deviation to the White Tower is not possible, as the access road has 'private' notices.) Continue round the coast, past some holiday homes. You can cut in front of almost all the buildings on the sea side, but in a few places you'll have to follow the wide track behind the buildings. Soon you reach **Armier Bay** (Picnic 4c), in summer a popular holiday area for the Maltese, where you can sample some restaurants and bars.

Ignoring the road to the crest of the ridge, cut across the headland of **Ta' Macca** (signposted 'RAMLA IL-QORTIN'), past more summer homes, and go on into **Ramlet il-Qortin**. Follow the beach past colourful boathouses and arrive in front of the RAMLA BAY RESORT. Bear left past the main building and then right down a lane, to reach the waterfront near the old GOZO FERRY HARBOUR at **Marfa** (**2h25min**), now overlooked by the buildings of the RIVIERA RESORT HOTEL (which was being renovated at press date). Today boats belonging to diving schools and the ferry to Comino (Comino Ferries Co-op Ltd) are the main traffic from the port. A little further on is the PALAZZ TAL-MARFA (**2h30min**) on the main road to Cirkewwa, the present Gozo ferry terminal. Catch the bus at the stop (Ahrax) on the corner, next to the Palazz.

The Red Tower — a landmark on Marfa Ridge

Walk 5 MALTA: RED TOWER • QAMMIEH • IC-CUMNIJA • GHADIRA

See map pages 46-47; see also photographs pages 48-49, 52
Distance: 4.3km/2.7mi; 1h25min
Grade: easy, with ascents/descents of 120m/400ft overall
Equipment: stout shoes, sunhat, waterproofs, swimwear, picnic, water
How to get there: 🚌 41, 42 from Valletta (every 30min, journey time about 1h); 🚌 222 from Sliema (every 30min, journey time about 50min); 🚌 221 from Bugibba (every 30min, journey time about 25min). Alight at the junction near the Red Tower.
To return: 🚌 41, 42, 49 fro Ghadira to Valletta

Alternative walk: Red Towe Qammieh — Cirkewwa
(4.5km/2.8mi; 1h30min; eas with an ascent of 70m/225ft descent of 120m/400ft). Foll the main walk to the old rac station at Qammieh. Retrac your steps for about 100m/y after passing the last of the disused buildings, then take track on the left and follow above the cliffs to Paradise Take the road to Cirkewwa catch a bus at the stop oppo the hotel.

This walk is about ridges and valleys, white cliffs, aqu marine sea and Second World War relics. The vie from the western end of the Marfa Ridge are among t best on Malta.

The walk begins at QAMMIEH ROUNDABOUT near the summit of **Marfa Ridge**. **Start out** by taking the small road running west and, after a short climb to the crest of the ridge, pass the 17th-century **Red Tower (5min; Picnic 5)** on your right — a historic monument and military post (the varying opening hours are displayed on a noticeboard; there is a small entrance fee). Enjoy the fine views, taking in both the north and east coasts of Malta and extending all the way to Comino and Gozo. At **20min** a honey-coloured wall supporting the edge of a lay-by is visible on the left-hand side of the road; note this landmark for your return. Proceed straight along the road, following the crest of the ridge and enjoying the magnificent scenery and cooling breezes.

At **35min**, above the **Qammieh Cliffs**, lie the remains of a RADIO STATION built by the Americans. From here retrace your route and in 15 minutes (**50min**) come to a path on your right some 30m/yds east of the lay-by (already described at the 20min-point) which leads to a set of rough steps. The steps descend to a steep footpath with a rather loose surface. It continues past abandoned terraces and comes to a track.

Here turn left, passing the head of the spectacular inlet shown overleaf, **Ic-Cumnija** (The Chimney). At **1h** you reach two small PILLBOXES, from where the track becomes a narrow road leading downhill to a valley of irrigated fields, water tanks, windmills and farmhouses. You'll more than likely see people working their fields or a shepherd herding his flock on the higher ground.

At the junction with the VALLEY ROAD (**1h10min**) turn left towards the coast (by a farm building and a couple of irrigation tanks). After five minutes (**1h15min**) bear right on a track (where the road begins to go uphill) and follow this to a group of Maltese holiday homes. You meet the main Mellieha/Cirkewwa road opposite the entrance to the MELLIEHA BAY RESORT HOTEL. Catch a bus (for either direction) on the right here (Riserva bus stop) or in a few minutes arrive at **Mellieha Bay** — one of Malta's most popular beaches. Cool off and then catch a bus from one of the bus stops on the promenade at **Ghadira (1h25min)**.

Alternative walk 5: the western edge of Marfa Ridge, with the Paradise Bay Resort Hotel and Comino in the background

Walk 6 MALTA: GHADIRA • IL PRAJJIET • GHAJN SNUBER • GOLDEN BAY

Distance: 7.2km/4.5mi; 2h20min

Grade: easy initially, then moderate, with some scrambling around Ghajn Snuber and Ras il-Wahx. Overall ascent of 120m/400ft and descent of 100m/325ft.

Equipment: stout shoes, sunhat, swimwear, waterproofs, picnic, water

How to get there: 🚐 41, 42 from Valletta (every 30min, journey time about 1h); 🚐 222 from Sliema (every 30min, journey time about 50min); 🚐 221 from Bugibba (every 30min, journey time 25min). Alight at the Riserva bus stop opposite the entrance to the Mellieha Bay Resort Hotel.

To return: 🚐 44 from Golden Bay to Valletta, 🚐 225 to Sliema, 🚐 223 to Bugibba

Alternative walk: Ghadira — Ghajn Snuber — Mizieb — Selmun (10km/6.2mi; 3h30min; grade as main walk, with an ascent of 120m/400ft and descent of 60m/200ft). Follow the main walk to Ghajn Snuber tower and walk back to the sharp bend on the Manikata/Mellieha secondary road. Follow the road downhill into the Mizieb Valley. Opposite a group of farm buildings, take a track on the left to Mizieb pumping station. (Now refer to the map on pages 58-59.) In another 7min turn right onto a road; then, in 60m/yds, go left on a track which follows the valley. Continue straight on to the St Paul's Bay/Mellieha road near Selmun. Turn right for bus stops in both directions.

This walk begins and ends near sandy beaches. It also visits the 'Popeye Village', where the old film set and the Children's World theme park are the main attractions. As in Walk 5, you will also come upon ridges, valleys and former military installations.

The walk begins near where Walk 5 ends — at the **Riserva** bus stop opposite the entrance to the MELLIEHA BAY RESORT HOTEL. Ignore the entrance to the caravan and second home site on the left and take the next left turn, beside a tall pillar and telephone box. At the start your way is tree-lined and flanked by a high wall on the right and holiday homes on your left. Pass a run-down *bocci* pitch and descend slightly, to a track coming from the holiday homes (**5min**); this is the 1h15min-point on Walk 5. In two minutes ignore the left fork leading into fields and carry straight on, reaching the point where Walk 5 comes down from the ridge on your right (**10min**). Once again keep straight ahead until the road bends left downhill (**13min**) towards the gates of the NORTH WEST WATER TREATMENT PLANT, where you turn left then right around the perimeter.

After about **17min** the road ends and a brown earthen path lies ahead. Sometimes vehicles parked here obscure the view of the start of the path — which should show up as a distinctive brown colour against the grey/white limestone in the rough terrain as it climbs towards a gap between two low hills. In five minutes (**22min**) cross a stream where there is a walled enclosure and a SHOOTER'S HUT on the right.

The top of the ridge is gained in about ten minutes, and you are now on the **Ras in-Niexfa** (Arid Point; **30min**). From here you look out towards the next part of your walk, the Qasam Barani, an isolated and desolate area, which is uninhabited except for the Devil's Farmhouse. Descend from the ridge towards a narrow fjord-like inlet, **Il-Prajjiet** (Anchor Bay; **40min**). Once a lovely secluded spot, this bay was converted into an 18th-century port for the film 'Popeye'. There used to be a lovely cliff-edge path here, but it is now impassable. Instead, make your way to the eastern perimeter or the site, where there is a clump of bamboo and an old storage building. Follow a faint path downhill, between the bamboo on the right and the storage building on the left. In one minute you reach a track coming from plastic-covered greenhouses which takes you to a road from Ghadira and the Mellieha by-pass.

Turn right and pass in front of the entrance to the CHILDREN'S WORLD AND POPEYE VILLAGE theme park, where there is a bus stop (Bus 101 between Cirkewwa and Mgarr). Follow the road southwest round Il-Prajjiet and take the first road on the left. This passes fields protected by cane windbreaks and then becomes an eroded track as it sharply climbs the north face of the Mellieha Ridge. The going becomes easier as the last of the terraced fields are left behind. A PILLBOX adjacent to the parallel road to the left can be seen in the distance at **55min**.

In about 10 minutes the track exits at a sharp bend on the MELLIEHA/MANIKATA ROAD (**1h05min**). Turn right here on a track which leads in a little over five minutes to the **Ghajn Snuber Tower** (**1h12min**). Wild thyme, wolfbane, rock-samphire, giant hyacinth

Left: Ic-Cumnija, from the Qammieh Cliffs (Walk 5). Walk 6 follows a route just to the south of the headland in the middle distance.

(*Urginea maritima*), and the late-flowering *Narcissus serotinus* make this setting a real paradise for botanists. Ghajn Snuber ('Spring by the Aleppo Pines') was a military training ground; sadly, the pines have gone.

Walk down towards the cliff-edge, which is reached by

following a walled-in track. An old building lies 200m/yds over to your left. A small building at the edge of the cliff is your goal. When you get there, turn left, and after 80m/yds discover a STAIRWAY in the cliff, leading down to two huts with circular walled gardens. The walk now turns south, following the edge

'Popeye Village'— the old film set is still a tourist attraction.

of the cliff (but not *too* closely). At the end of the main cliff path, in just under **1h35min**, follow a red earthen track for some 50m/yds, passing to the right of a small stone hut. From the top of the ridge it is easy to see how the rocky headland came by its fearsome name, Horror Point, where a gun emplacement in a dangerous condition is cut into the cliffs (**Ras il-Wahx**; **1h45min**).

Return to the cliff-edge, passing a spring which feeds the little plots below. Golden Bay and the old naval rifle range are in the foreground. At the **2h**-point you pass a small ruined war-time FORTIFICATION and a modern walled enclosure on your left. About one minute past here, a track rises from the undercliff on your right (at another disused military building). Bear round to the left, ignoring another track on the right. Ahead is a large wall (partly collapsed). The track skirts round the left-hand side of this wall and crosses a little valley. In a further minute, ignore a track on your right.

You come to a Rural Heritage Project (www.manikatafarmers. com) involving an historic farmstead, Roman tombs, a World War II military post and indigenous trees and plants. In a minute, on entering the outskirts of **Manikata** on a street known as Triq Mejjiesa (**2h10min**), walk past new houses for some 300m/yds, then turn right downhill on a recently widened road. In no more than three minutes, at a WATER TANK AND FARM, turn right. Almost immediately, go straight ahead (the left turn leads across the Pwales Valley), passing a converted farmhouse on the right.

Take care here, as this road is now a bus route for buses 44 and 101 heading to the terminus at Golden Bay. Pass the entrance to the OLD MILITARY BASE on your right and in another two minutes, just after another disused military structure, turn right towards the GOLDEN SANDS RESORT and the BUS TERMINUS at **Golden Bay** (Picnic 6b; just over **2h20min**).

Walk 7 MALTA: MELLIEHA • SELMUN PALACE • MGIEBAH VALLEY • BLATA L-BAJDA • MISTRA BAY • XEMXIJA

See also photographs pages 12, 13

Distance: 8.3km/5.2mi; 2h

Grade: quite easy except for the fairy difficult descent after the 45min-point; ascent 145m/475ft; descent 200m/650ft

Equipment: stout shoes, sunhat, swimwear, waterproofs, picnic, water

How to get there: 🚌 41, 42, 221, 222, X1 to Mellieha bus stop (near the entrance to Mellieha village; see map overleaf); journey time 45min
To return: 🚌 41, 42 to Valletta

Short walk 1: Selmun Palace — Mgiebah Bay — Selmun Palace (3.2km/2mi; 50min; easy, with an ascent/descent of 100m/350ft). Follow the main walk down the Mgiebah Valley to the bay and return the same way.

Short walk 2: Selmun Palace — Blata l-Bajda — Selmun Palace (4km/2.5mi; 1h; easy, level walking). Take the road from the palace out to Fort Campbell and follow the main walk from the 45min-point to the 1h05min-point; return the same way.

Short walk 3: Selmun Palace — Mistra Bay — Xemxija (1.5km/0.9mi; 45min; easy, with an ascent of 25m/75ft and descent of 90m/300ft). Bear right around Selmun Palace, then turn right on a track. In 50m/yds, turn left on a track/path that heads straight downhill. When you meet the valley road, turn left to Mistra Bay. See page 59 to follow the main walk (either by road or path) to the bus stop outside Xemxija.

The start of this ramble, at a roundabout near a housing estate on the outskirts of Mellieha, may be a little uninspiring! Don't despair; a British fort, a Portuguese redoubt, secret valleys, and delightful coves combine to make this one of Malta's best medium-distance walks.

Set off from the **roundabout** on the St Paul's Bay/Mellieha road in the direction of 'Selmun Palace Hotel'. The road passes through the hamlet of **Selmun** (Picnic 7a), and the baroque-style **Selmun Palace**, bearing the arms of the Monte di Renden-zione, is reached in 1km. From the palace tower walk left, following a track that skirts a small farm building. When you come to a crossroads (**15min**), turn right and follow the small road winding down into the **Mgiebah Valley**. This hidden little valley overflows with market garden produce and is one of the last places where the holm oak (*Quercus ilex*), which once covered the islands, still grows. In winter it resounds to the rush of tinkling water in the stone irrigation channels.

On reaching a FARMHOUSE (**25min**), turn right to cross the valley. (Just after turning, a diversion may be made to Mgiebah Bay for Picnic 7b or a swim by following the valley to the sea.) Two minutes past the farm, head right again, following a very narrow path flanked by thorn bushes. You pass another small farm building. Two minutes later, turn left on a small road. This passes through tiny walled-in fields. At about the **31min**-mark,

56

where the road twists to the left, turn right uphill on a path between walls. This widens into a track and in two minutes (**33min**) exits on the road from Selmun Palace to Fort Campbell. Turn left here, in seven minutes reaching **Fort Campbell** (**40min**). This coastal battery was built in 1936. A left turn takes you between the old fort buildings (keep the outer wall on your right).

At **45min**, at a sharp left-hand bend in the road, turn right on the lower of two dirt tracks and slither down the clay slopes to the salt pans at **Blata l-Bajda** (**1h**; photograph page 13). The blinding-white rock, indigo sea, and salty spray are exhilarating. Soon a fine viewpoint overlooking the islets of St Paul's, complete with a statue to commemorate the reputed shipwreck of St Paul in 60AD (the statue is more modern), stops you in your tracks. The coastal path takes you to a GUN TOWER and then a manhole access to a cliff LOOKOUT that has been sealed with a concrete cap (**1h15min**).

Climb more steeply up to **Rdum il-Bies** (Cliffs of the Hawks) and around **Ras il-Mignuna** (Mad Point); then descend to the **Pinto Redoubt**, which stands guard over **Mistra Bay**. This is a fine setting for a swim and Picnic 7c.

Mistra Valley

Follow the road for a final ascent through a valley* rich in agriculture. On meeting the MAIN ROAD (**2h**), turn left for the bus stop (Mistra) on the outskirts of **Xemxija**.

*Alternative end: where the road begins to climb up the valley, turn left on the beach, keeping a group of buildings on your right. In under a minute, take a path/stone steps straight up off the beach. Pass an old quarry on your right (5min) and, two minutes later, bear right towards a walled enclosure. From the enclosure follow the track to a roundabout on the outskirts of Xemxija (12min). Turn left to find bus stops (Xemxija) in both directions less than 100m/yds along.

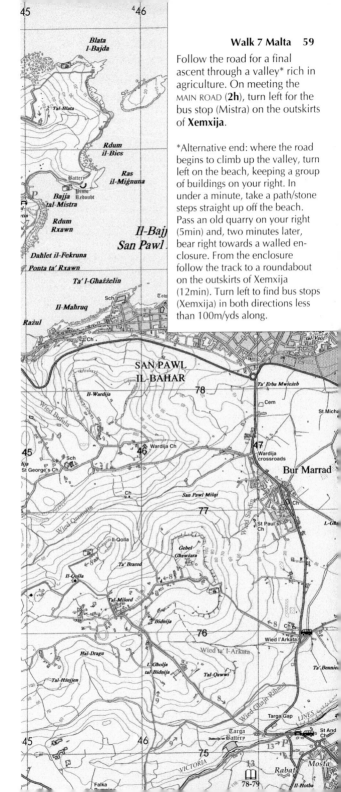

Walk 8 MALTA: WIED L-ARKATA • BIDNIJA • IL-QOLLA • PWALES VALLEY • XEMXIJA

See map pages 58-59
Distance: 9.4km/5.9mi; 2h35min
Grade: easy, with an overall ascent/descent of 190m/625ft
Equipment: stout shoes, sunhat, waterproofs, picnic, water
How to get there: 🚌 41, 42 from Valletta; alight at Rihana, the first stop past Targa Gap
To return: 🚌 41, 42 from Roti (Xemxija) to Valletta.

Short walk: Wied l-Arkata — Bidnija — Targa Gap
(4km/2.5mi; 1h15min; easy, with an ascent of 100m/325ft). Follow the main walk to Bidnija, turn left just past the church and take the small road back to the main road (it comes out on the hairpin bend at Targa Gap). Return by 🚌 41, 42 to Valletta from the public garden on the outskirts of Mosta (a few minutes east of the hairpin bend).

Inland Malta at its best is explored on this walk, which begins and ends at picturesque chapels. You visit Bronze Age sites, interesting farm buildings and an intimate steep-sided valley. There are panoramic views throughout.

Begin at Wied l-Arkata: head in a westerly direction on a narrow road left of the CHAPEL (sign-posted 'TRIQ GĦAJN RIHANA'). This becomes a track after 100m/yds. After passing several houses, you gradually climb between fields. After **15min**, where there is a gate into a field, turn left uphill and follow a rocky, overgrown trail up the hill, past abandoned terraces. In five minutes you come onto a road: follow it through the charming tucked-away village

of **Bidnija**, to the church (**35min**). It's very quiet here; there is little traffic, and just one small shop.

Past the church, turn right into TRIQ IL-BDIEWA and, in a few minutes, turn left at a large GATE WITH PILLARS, ignoring the narrow lane that leads into the valley. At just over **40min**, at a restored FARMHOUSE, take the right-hand fork. In a few minutes, turn 90° to the right. Your goal is now the flat-topped circular rock know as **Il-Qolla** (The Fat-Bellied Jug). Unfortunately a 'Private' sign has appeared at the start of the path up to the summit; however, there are still fine views to be enjoyed in the vicinity of Il-Qolla.

Now retrace your steps to the farmhouse, turn right on an old cart-track and, in a few minutes, turn right again. At about **1h10min** a CLUB-HOUSE FOR CLAY-PIGEON SHOOTERS is reached. Go straight ahead on a narrow earth-surfaced lane which in 100m/yds turns 90° to the left and winds along the cliff-line

Bidnija church

Pwales Valley

above a watercourse (the **Wied Qannotta**).

After five minutes you pass a farm on your left: go straight ahead at this point, to avoid the descent into the steepest part of the valley and the climb back up. You pass a house and, one minute later keep straight on, soon coming to the SANTA MARIJA FIREWORKS FACTORY (**1h24min**). A few minutes later, follow the main track round to the right — to the RIDGE ROAD coming from Wardija (**1h30min**), where there are some fine views.

The next section sees some easy walking. Turn left on the road, and turn right on the ST PAUL'S BAY/ZEBBIEH ROAD (**1h37min**). This takes you past a little SHRINE in a grotto, hidden behind gates, where there are seats in the shade. Two minutes later you come to the entrance to the VILLA SAN MARTIN, beyond which you are descending into the **Pwales Valley**. Strolling along, relish the views stretching down to St Paul's Bay.

You meet the ST PAUL'S BAY/ GOLDEN BAY ROAD at **2h10min**.

Cross the road and take the MIZIEB ROAD straight ahead, to the hamlet of **L'Imbordin** (**2h20min**). Continue as far as the last house on your left (ANTONIA HOUSE) and go right here on a narrow track flanked by bamboo. In about a minute this becomes a trail between stone walls. In another minute pass a room cut into the rock face and 100m/yds further on come to a small CHAPEL AND TWO STATUES (**2h23min**).

The track twists downhill, acquires a concrete surface, and becomes a minor road passing a succession of farmhouses overlooking the **Pwales Valley**. At around the **2h28min**-mark you come to a junction with farm tracks: turn right and then left (after no more than 60m/yds, at a small WATER SERVICES DEPOT). The road passes the **Is-Simar Nature Reserve** and leads to the outskirts of **Xemxija**. You reach the MAIN ROAD and promenade some 75m/yds south of the PORTO DEL SOL GUEST HOUSE, where there are bus stops (Roti) for both directions (**2h35min**).

Walk 9 MALTA: FALKA • WIED IL-GHAJN RIHANA • GHALLIS TOWER

Distance: 7km/4.4mi; 2h10min
Grade: easy, but there is a rough descent at the start, and some of the cart-tracks are muddy after rain. Ascent 40m/125ft; descent 145m/475ft
Equipment: stout shoes, sunhat, waterproofs, picnic, water
How to get there: 🚌 44 from Valletta to Mgarr/Golden Bay (departures every 30 minutes; journey time about 40 minutes); alight at the stop 100m/yds west of the Ta' Falka pumping station on the Mosta/Mgarr road (Hzejjen bus stop).
To return: 🚕 either arrange for a taxi to pick you up at the Tower

or retrace your steps to the main road near the Villa Trevi where there is a bus stop (Mejjieli) served by Bus 49 at 40min past each hour (last bus 21.40) in the direction of Naxxar and Valletta; if you are travelling to Bugibba or Mellieha you should be at the stop no later than 30min past the hour, although at busy times of the day the bus is likely to be 5-10min later.

Short walk: Falka — Wied l-Arkata
(2.4km/1.5mi; 40min; easy, with a descent of 85m/275ft). Follow the main walk from the Falka pumping station to the little stone bridge on the St Paul's Bay/Mosta road (🚌 31, 41, 42).

Alternative walk: Falka — Bidnija — Xemxija (8.8km/5.5mi; 2h50min; grade as main walk, but an ascent of 130m/425ft and descent of 230m/750ft). Follow the main walk to the ford (20min). Continue straight ahead uphill on a track, to the Mosta/Bidnija road (30min). Turn left into Bidnija and the church shown on page 60 (35min). Now follow Walk 8 from the 35min-point.

O n this easy stroll you will only climb one low hill, and effortlessly take in some of Malta's pleasant rural scenery.

Begin the walk at the TA' FALKA PUMPING STATION, with its large blue-painted gates. Take the small road heading northeast, by a farmhouse. In **5min** turn left on a concreted farm track which leads down to the floor of the **Wied il-Ghajn Rihana (16min)**. Continue straight on (just before a ruined hut and VINEYARD). Four minutes later, ford a stream (**20min**) and immediately turn right on another track, past a small DAM. Meeting another track, turn right to the MOSTA/ BIDNIJA ROAD (**30min**). Cross the road and keep to the right-hand side of the valley.* Shortly afterwards, at another DAM, cross to the left-hand side of the valley, on a narrow path skirting the fields shown overleaf.

A third DAM comes up at **40min**. Turn right and cross over it. A well-trodden path at the edge of a field leads past vines, then rises to another field at a small building with a metal door. From here follow a track for 100m/yds to the busy St Paul's Bay/Mosta road at **Wied l-Arkata** (**43min**), where Walk 8 begins.

Turn left, taking advantage of the pavement, and after 400m/yds, cross the road and take a minor road on your right

*A gate has been erected here, and if it is locked you should turn left and follow the road into Bidnija and use the notes on page 60 to follow Walk 10 in reverse to Wied l'Arkata where you can resume the walk at about the 45min-point.

Nearing a bridge over the water-course, on the Mosta/Bidnija road

cart-track (a short stretch of which is prone to flooding after heavy rain), you soon overlook Salina Bay. The 17th-century **Ghallis Tower** (built by Grand Master Martin de Redin; **2h10min**) marks the end of the walk.

Unfortunately, when the coast road was recently upgraded to a dual carriageway, no provision was made for a pelican crossing to access the wide coastal promenade. It would be very dangerous to attempt to walk on the carriageway to the nearest bus stops (at the Salini Resort, about 1km in the direction of Bugibba), so you should either telephone for a taxi or walk back to the stop for Bus 49 on the road near Villa Trevi.

that runs parallel with the *wied*. In just over **1h** ignore a right turn at IL-BARRIERA farmhouse and almost immediately cross another *wied* (**Il-Ghasel**).

Go straight across the SAN PAWL TAT-TARGA/BUR MARRAD ROAD (**1h10min**) and at a three-way fork keep straight ahead on an old trail between stone walls. This rises to **Il-Qadi** (55m/175ft). After fifteen minutes, at a T-junction by a large new farm building with wide gates on rollers, turn right on a track (named TRIQ TAL-QADI at the next junction). Emerging on the SAN PAWL TAT-TARGA/SALINA BAY ROAD, turn right again. Note that there is a bus stop (Mejjieli) for Bus 49 here. A couple of minutes later, turn left on a road at VILLA TREVI, in just over two minutes passing NEG NEG FARM on your right.

You are now on the RIDGE TRAIL, heading for the shimmering Mediterranean, with fine views on both sides. The wide fields give way to flat, open, rocky land, the *misrah*. Following a

Walk 10 MALTA: ST ANDREW'S • MADLIENA • GHARGHUR • MAGHTAB • BAHAR IC-CAGHAQ

Distance: 7.7km/4.8mi; 1h45min

Grade: generally easy; a moderate ascent to Madliena and another towards Gharghur. Overall ascent/descent of 170m/550ft

Equipment: stout shoes, sunhat, swimwear, waterproofs, picnic, water

How to get there: 🚌 13, 14 from Valletta to Pembroke Park and Ride bus stop, St Andrew's

— about 150m/yds east of the junction with Triq Ta'L-Ibrag (departures every 5-10 minutes; journey time about 35min). *To return:* 🚌 13 from Bahar ic-Caghaq to Bugibba and Sliema

Short walk: St Andrew's — Gharghur (5.3km/3.3mi; 1h10min; grade as main walk). Follow the main walk to Gharghur and catch 🚌 46 to Valletta.

This unusual walk begins at traffic lights in the St Andrew's district, on the coastal road to/from St Julian's. Leaving the busy main road, the route goes through one of Malta's most sought-after residential areas, before visiting a peaceful hilltop village with spectacular views.

Start out by walking uphill on TRIQ TA'L-IBRAG, a busy street with many small shops. In **10min** pass the HALLAND HOTEL

(now closed). Continue straight on, passing a small fortified TOWER and coming to a T-junction just under three

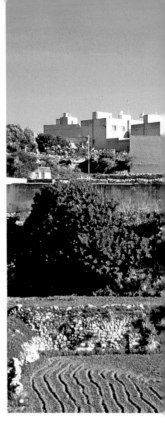

Right: This 16th-century chapel dedicated to the Assumption of Our Lady rises above carefully tended terraces at Gharghur. There are over 300 churches and chapels on Malta, many of the latter in the countryside — built for farmers who were too far from the urban centres for daily prayer.

minutes later. Turn right into Triq Madliena (by two houses called Antonia and Caro Cottage).

After passing two old quarries and a converted farmhouse (Sedona Farmhouse) and two old quarries, your way descends straight ahead into **Madliena** (**25min**). Carry straight on at a wide junction next to the Mystique nightclub and several villas. You pass some fine old country houses near the junction with Triq il-Bir, where you proceed straight ahead. Pass a small church on the left at the **40min** mark; just beyond it, there are several farmhouses on both sides of the road, some of which have been converted into villas. Just beyond these is a fine view of the Madliena Valley overlooked by Fort Madliena

66

(built by the British in 1880 and still in use by the military).

Ignore the left turn (Triq Wied id-Dis) and, in less than a minute, pass Villa Madalena. Then follow a path on the left leading downhill beside a broken-away wall and a line of telegraph poles. The path takes you to an avenue flanked by yet more villas and the Madliena Village Apartments. Continue downhill, turn left at the T-junction, and cross the bridge over the **Wied id-Dis** (**50min**).

Follow the quiet road towards the village of Gharghur. In about 10 minutes you pass a house on the left with a long garden. An inscription in Italian commemorates its housing of the British commanders of the village garrison during the reign of King George III. Some 100m/yds further on, you come to a well-kept chapel built in 1560 and dedicated to the **Assumption of Our Lady**. The next landmark, only another 100m/yds further along, is a modern house known as VILLA SUZIE.

Continue straight on into TRIQ IL-GNIEN and, almost immediately, turn right into TRIQ GHAXQET L-GHAJN. (If you turn left at Villa Suzie, then right at the next junction, this would take you to **Gharghur** church and the village centre, where there are shops and bars — a detour of under five minutes each way.) From Triq Ghaxqet L-Ghajn you enjoy the fine view of the Assumption Chapel shown above. In just under ten minutes you reach the **Victoria Lines**

(**1h05min**; Picnic 10a), where there are superb views stretching from the Maghtab Plain below to St Paul's Bay, Comino, and even the dome of Xewkija's church on Gozo. The Lines (see photograph opposite) were built by the British between 1870 and 1899 on a high ridge, to protect Valletta and other towns around the Grand Harbour from enemy landings on the north side of the island.

The Lines are your route for just under ten minutes, until you meet a road. There is a small GARDEN together with seats at this point (Picnic 10b). Turn right here (TRIQ GHAR SAN BRINKAT) and descend on an asphalt road to the **Maghtab** plain (passing a farm on the left). Continue to a T-junction at a

The Victoria lines, near the end of the walk, were built to protect Valletta and other towns around the Grand Harbour, shown above. At the top is a view to Senglea from the Post of France, below a view to Fort St Angelo (Vittoriosa) from near the Upper Barracca Gardens.

house called IL-BEJTA (**1h35min**) and turn right into TRIQ SANTA KLARA. Pass the VILLA TAL-FANAL, the usually dry watercourse, and an old wartime NISSAN HUT. Just after passing an unnamed farm building, take the right-hand fork and at **St John's Church** (**1h40min**), turn left on TRIQ SAN GWANN L'EVANGELISTA and in two minutes meet the

coast road opposite the **Mediterraneo Water Park** at **Bahar ic-Caghaq** (**1h45min**). The park offers the opportunity to try swimming with dolphins, should you fancy a change from walking! About 150m/yds towards Bugibba there are bus stops in both directions, as well as a small bar for those in need of refreshment.

Walk 11 MALTA: BINGEMMA GAP • NADUR TOWER • BINGEMMA FORT • L-ISKORVIT • GHAJN TUFFIEHA

Distance: 7.6km/4.8mi; 2h15min

Grade: mainly easy, with rougher walking along the cliffs and a rutted path towards Ghajn Tuffieha; ascent of 70m/225ft and descent of 240m/775ft

Equipment: stout shoes, sunhat, swimwear, waterproofs, picnic, water

How to get there: 🚌 51, 52, 53 from Valletta to Rabat interchange. Departures every 10 minutes; journey time about 40min. Change to 🚌 109 to Santi bus stop. Departures every hour; journey time about 35min. Walk 5min to Bingemma Gap.

To return: 🚌 44 from Ghajn Tuffieha (Riviera bus stop) to Valletta

Short walk 1: Bingemma Gap — Tas-Santi — Bingemma Gap (7.4km/4.6mi; 1h40min; easy, with an overall ascent/descent of 150m/500ft). 🚌 109 to/from Santi. From Santi walk 5min to the chapel at Bingemma Gap. Follow the main walk through Tas-Santi and, 100m/yds after passing a bus shelter on the left, take the next minor road on the right. Continue for about 10min, then turn left and immediately right (at a stone pillar). In 5min you reach Bingemma hamlet, where a shrine marks your right turn along another minor road — back to Bingemma Gap.

Short walk 2: Mgarr — Ghajn Tuffieha (3.6km/2.3mi; 55min; grade as main walk). From Mgarr Church (🚌 44) go west on the Gnejna road and join the main walk by turning right at the crossroads beyond the house called Zammitello Palace (the 1h25min-point in the main walk).

Western Malta at its best — a Roman cemetery, a British fort, watchtowers, a lovely cultivated valley, and — finally — spectacular coastal scenery to end your ramble.

Start at the CHAPEL at **Bingemma Gap** (Picnic 11a): facing south (the way you've come): you will see on your left some rock-hewn tombs, reputed to be a ROMAN CEMETERY. Also on this side of the valley are the **Dwejra Lines** (part of the Victoria Lines, setting for Walk 13). Walk south down the quiet narrow road and, in **5min**,

The Victoria Lines at Bingemma Gap

View northeast from the Victoria Lines

turn right at a crossroads. **Nadur Tower** (240m/785ft) is reached in **15min** — one of the highest points on Malta.

From the tower, bear right down a minor road which leads to a farmhouse (**21min**). Just after passing to the left of the farm, ignore the track continuing downhill; instead take a footpath on your left. The path offers some superb views of northern Malta and Gozo as it follows the **Victoria Lines** to **Bingemma Fort** (**30min**). This Victorian fort, which saw action in World War

II, retains its original coat of arms and drawbridge. The slopes below may be full of wild asparagus in spring.

Skirt the ditch and follow the access road south. Ignore the first right turn (there is a 'no through road' sign on this small road). In three minutes (**33min**) almost opposite a farmhouse, turn right. This narrow road takes you gently downhill. Ignore a small road on the right almost at once (also marked by a 'no through road' sign). This pleasant secondary road drops steadily through the **Tas-Santi Gap**. There are fine views over the terraced fields to the coast and as far north as Gozo.

At **1h05min** pass through the quiet hamlet of **L-Iskorvit**. Cross the MGARR/GNEJNA BAY ROAD (**1h25min**) and, in five minutes (at the top of the rise), take the stony track off left, just beyond a new house with lights either side of a high wrought-iron gate. Zammitello Palace (a country house masquerading as a palace) is perched on the hillside to your right. Soon you're at **Lippija Tower** (**1h45min**; Picnic 11b), standing guard over **Gnejna Bay**. You have breathtaking views across to Il-Pellegrin (The Wanderer). From here take the footpath along the cliff (*not* too close to the edge; rockfalls are frequent in wet weather). You look down on Flat-Rock Bay and the Dinosaur — the peculiar ridge of blue clay that connects the ridge you're walking with Il-Karraba (The Battleship). Where a field wall comes in from the right (**2h**), take a path on the left. This becomes a track and passes several derelict buildings before reaching **Ghajn Tuffieha Bay** (**2h15min**). The BUS STOP (Riviera) is on your right.

Walk 12 MALTA: MTARFA (ANTOINE) • CHADWICK LAKES • MTAHLEB • IL-QLEJGHA • BAHRIJA • KUNCIZZJONI • MGARR

See also photograph on page 28
Distance: 15.2km/9.5mi; 3h50min
Grade: generally easy, but the descents towards Fomm ir-Rih and Gnejna are steep and have been rutted in places by scrambler bikes; sure-footedness and a head for heights are essential. Ascent of 140m/450ft and descent of 300m/1000ft
Equipment: stout shoes, walking stick(s), sunhat, swimwear, waterproofs, picnic, water
How to get there: 🚌 51 from Valletta to Mtarfa, or (in wet weather) 🚌 51/53 to Gargir bus stop in Rabat's Nigred Housing Estate. Departures every 30min; journey time about 55min.
To return: 🚌 44 from Mgarr to Valletta

Short walk 1: Mtarfa (Antoine) — Chadwick Lakes — Fiddien Bridge — Rabat (Busugrilla) (3.5km/2.2mi; 45min; easy, with ascent/descent of 60m/200ft). Follow the main walk as far as Fiddien Bridge and return via the 'wet weather route' in reverse (see map).
Short walk 2: Mtarfa (Antoine) — Chadwick Lakes — Fiddien Bridge — Mtahleb — Il-Qlejgha — Bahrija (8km/5mi; 2h; easy, with an ascent/descent of 90m/300ft). Follow the main walk to the centre of Bahrija and catch 🚌 109 to Rabat.
Alternative walk 1: Mtarfa (Antoine) — Chadwick Lakes — Dwejra Lines — Mosta (7.8km/4.9mi; 2h10min; easy, with an ascent of 60m/200ft and descent of 175m/575ft). Follow the main walk to the Chadwick Lakes and cross the bridge (15min). Then turn right and immediately left, picking up Walk 13 at the 1h10min point. Return as Walk 13.
Alternative walk 2: Mtarfa (Antoine) — Chadwick Lakes — Ghemieri Bridge — Ghemieri — Tas Santi — Mgarr (9.4km/5.9mi); 2h40min; easy, with an ascent of 115m/375ft and descent of 200m/650ft). Follow the main walk to the Chadwick Lakes and cross the bridge (15min). Then turn left and proceed to just before the Rabat/Ghemieri road bridge (40min). Turn right up a track immediately before the bridge, to reach the road, and then turn right. Follow this past the Fiddien booster pumping station. After a gentle climb, take a concrete track on your right to Ghemieri (45min). Go straight through this hamlet, to a T-junction (1h). Turn left at a house called Orangeville. After a few metres/yards, at a shelter where the road bends to the left, take a rough track descending between stone walls. This exits on a road coming from Bingemma Fort (1h05min). Go straight ahead here, then pick up Walk 11 at the 33min-point (almost opposite a farmhouse) and follow it to the end.

S tarting on the outskirts of Mtarfa near Rabat, this walk visits the Chadwick Lakes irrigation system and remote hamlets before exploring some of Malta's most spectacular cliff scenery. The closing stretch takes in much of the island's best farmland and one of its least spoilt villages.

The Qlejgha Valley near Ghemieri Bridge

In fine weather,* the walk starts at the first bus stop (Antoine) on TRIQ ANTOINE DEBONO in **Mtarfa**. Turn left immediately, and soon the narrow road plunges downhill to the floor of the **Qlejgha Valley**. Cross the bridge over one of the **Chadwick Lakes** (**10min**) and turn left. After about two minutes you pass a retaining wall (to prevent erosion damage). Bear left now, on the lower track beside the *wied*. Pass another BRIDGE AND DAM, beyond which the track merges with the bed of the *wied* (about **17min**). You reach the FINAL DAM a minute later. Steps here take you up to a path running parallel with the increasingly narrow river bed. Continue by walking under a BRIDGE carrying the RABAT/TAS SALIB/BINGEMMA GAP road. A small tributary joins you from the right (**Wied Ghomor; 25min**). Soon afterwards you pass under the RABAT/GHEMIERI ROAD BRIDGE. There is more reconstruction work ahead, including a STEEL FOOTBRIDGE which looks very out of character with the surrounding landscape — it might even have been 'borrowed' from a harbour or canal. Don't be tempted to cross it to the other bank; instead, continue on the left bank, soon bearing left at a small field and wind-pump, to reach the RABAT/MTAHLEB ROAD at **Fiddien Bridge** (**35min**). Turn right; on the far side of the bridge you come upon a small picnic area and a plaque commemorating the inauguration of the project by the Prime Minister on 12 December 1997. So far the walk has been mainly in the intimate confines of one of Malta's deeper river valley systems. The vistas begin to open up as you bear left following a signpost to 'IMTAHLEB' and 'LANDRIJIET' (where the right turn leads to Bahrija). Ignore all minor roads right and left, including one to Dingli (and Walk 14) which comes up in about 20 minutes (**55min**).

You arrive at **Mtahleb** (**1h15min**), a remote little village comprised of a church perched on the cliff-edge, an abandoned school that has now acquired a new lease of life as a 'CoRRS' (Centre of Residential Restorative Services), and a couple of houses. Don't take either of the

---

In wet weather,* alight from Bus 51 or 53 at the Gargir stop in the Nigred Housing Estate on the outskirts of Rabat and bear left along Triq Ghajn Kajjet. Follow the signs for Fiddien and you will reach **Fiddien Bridge in about **10min**. Pick up the main walk at the 35min-point.

left forks to the church; keep to the high ground. But in two minutes *do* fork left, on a narrow, barely-surfaced road along the plateau. Then bear right almost immediately, soon hugging the cliff-edge. Some 25 minutes from Mtahleb, continue straight on (ignoring the hairpin-bend road down to the coast). Ten minutes later (**1h50min**) you should be gazing at a long oval plateau, the site of a defensive Bronze Age village. In spring the area is a riot of wild flowers, but the spectacular views over northern Malta and Gozo can be enjoyed all year round.

Eventually the road, which has now become very narrow, peters out into a track and you bear right on another track, then right again, to descend into the **Wied Rini** (**2h**), where the narrow road leading into the small village of Bahrija is visible on the far side. There are many 'private' signs here, but they

refer to the fields and huts next to the track, not to the route itself. In just under five minutes you cross the watercourse and begin to climb out of the valley. The track meets the beginning of the road leading to Bahrija. A stiff three-minute climb follows. On entering **Bahrija** (**2h10min**), continue straight ahead (opposite a house called COUNTRY COTTAGE). Two minutes later ignore a road on the left which leads to a car park overlooking Fomm ir-Rih. It would be very dangerous to attempt a short-cut from the car park to the main walking route at the 3h10min-point. Continue straight ahead at a junction two minutes later. The BUS STOP, shops and several bars/restaurants in the centre of the village are reached in another minute. This remote community, once quite small, has grown as people escape the more congested areas.

Head out of the village on the

main road towards Rabat and, in 15 minutes (just after passing a RADIO MAST; **2h25min**), turn left, back towards the coast (signposted 'Kuncizzjoni'). Ten minutes later you pass the derelict ALCAZAR GUEST HOUSE, and in a further five minutes you reach the delightful church at **Kuncizzjoni** (**2h40min**), where an adjacent gate is inscribed 'Fondazione Paola 1731' — a reference to its founder, Grand Master Antione de Paule. Just before the church, turn right on a narrow road and in three minutes reach a VIEWPOINT where there is a MEMORIAL. Turn left here, going downhill past old military buildings on the right. At **2h35min** come to a pole barrier blocking vehicle access to these buildings. Bear left at another pole barrier and in two minutes arrive at the western end of the **Victoria Lines**. You pass a PILL-BOX set into the cliff-face (**2h55min**) and then squeeze into a narrow path

that descends steeply some 65m/200ft and follow this until you come to **Fomm ir-Rih Bay** (**3h10min**).

The path becomes a farm road for a short distance and passes a large irrigation tank. In about a minute, where it comes close to the cliff-edge overlooking the bay *(protected by a barrier, but keep a safe distance)*, there is a fine view of the headland known as **Ras ir-Raheb**. Turn right into a narrow road at a large farmhouse with boundary walls. The road winds its way through pleasant countryside and several hamlets, the second of which, **Ta' l-Abatija**, should be reached at around the **3h20min**-mark.

From here to Mgarr farming becomes more intensive, and an increasing proportion of crops are grown under plastic. The TAS-SANTI/MGARR ROAD is reached at about **3h27min**, where you turn left (Walk 11 joins here). Follow this for 20 minutes to a crossroads. Walk 11 goes straight on here, heading for the Lippija Tower and Golden Bay. A diversion can be made to Gnejna Bay by turning left (40 minutes return). Otherwise, turn right towards Mgarr with the main point of interest being the Castello Zammitello and its gardens, which boasts two matching conservatories. A further 10 minutes walking via TRIQ IL-KBIRA should be sufficient to reach the magnificent church at **Mgarr** — also known as the 'egg church': built over a long period, it was partly financed by the sale of eggs! There are BUS STOPS in both directions at the junction of TRIQ FISHER AND TRIQ SIR HARRY LUKE in front of the church (**3h50min**).

Walk 13 MALTA: MOSTA • QLEJGHA VALLEY • CHADWICK LAKES • DWEJRA LINES • MOSTA

See also photograph page 69
Distance: 11.2km/7mi; 3h05min
Grade: moderate, with some rough walking; overall ascent/descent of 115m/375ft
Equipment: stout shoes, sunhat, waterproofs, picnic, water
How to get there: 🚌 31, 41, 42 from Valletta to Mosta. Departures every 10min; journey time about 25min
To return: 🚌 31, 41, 42 to Valletta from the public garden at Targa Gap, on outskirts of Mosta

Short walk 1: Chadwick Lakes — Il-Qolla — Chadwick Lakes (4km/2.5mi; 1h; moderate, with an ascent/descent of 55m/175ft). 🚗 Only accessible by car: from the Busugrilla roundabout head northeast on the Mtarfa/Rabat bypass; the lakes are signposted on your left. Drive down the narrow road and turn right to a dam (limited parking). Follow the main walk from the 1h10min-point up to the road junction and turn right. After 400 metres (a quarter of a mile), turn right, taking a track parallel to the one you climbed up, to go back down to the Chadwick Lakes.

Short walk 2: Chadwick Lakes — Dwejra Lines — Chadwick Lakes (7.2km/4.5mi; 1h50min; moderate, with an ascent/descent of 60m/200ft). Access as Short walk 1 above. This option starts out as Short walk 1 above, but follows the main walk along the Dwejra Lines as far as the fort at the end. From there descend to the lower road and turn right. Come to a track on the left after 1.1km/0.7mi (the 'parallel track' in Short walk 1) and follow this down to the Chadwick Lakes and your car.

This is one of the classic walks on Malta, visiting the longest valley on the island, the famous Chadwick Lakes and the Dwejra Lines. Old forts and barracks provide added interest to a fascinating walk which offers magnificent panoramic views from the centre of the island.

The walk starts at Mosta Dome: follow Triq il-Kbira, passing near to the old Ta' Qali airfield. At **17min**, where the road forks, take the right-hand option (signposted 'Mgarr/Golden Bay'), and a few minutes later go right again, crossing the **Ta' L'Isperanza Valley** on an old bridge (**20min**) beside the delightful 18th-century chapel of **San Pawl tal-Qlejgha**. Come to a roundabout and follow signs for 'RABAT/MDINA', re-crossing the *wied*. Five minutes later, take a minor road on the right signposted 'Chadwick Lakes'. In another five minutes you should again cross the watercourse at the KARBUN BOREHOLE in the **Qlejgha Valley**. The meandering watercourse guides you below the old MTARFA BARRACKS and military hospital (now the site of a new town development), on the hill on your left — aptly named, as Mtarfa means 'Place on the Edge'.

Just as you're about level with Mtarfa, the first of the **Chadwick Lakes** appears (**1h**). Built in 1890 on the advice of Sir Robert Chadwick, to provide irrigation for San Anton Palace, they are quite an oddity in these parched islands. Three minutes later you cross a BRIDGE. In another

minute ignore a gated farm track and bridge on your left. Just past the SECOND DAM and *before* the THIRD BRIDGE (which Walk 12 crosses), take a narrow road at a prickly pear hedge on the right (**1h10min**). This becomes a grassy path at an ABANDONED FARM (**1h17min**). Ascend gradually through vineyards, where the hillock shown over-leaf (Il-Qolla) catches the eye. Near the top of the climb, beyond another farmhouse, go straight over a CROSSROADS (**1h35min**). In a few minutes, your track meets another road. Head for the little chapel at **Bingemma Gap** (Walk 11 has already been here), where there are fine views as far as Gozo. Retrace your steps and, after no more than two minutes, opposite a MILESTONE, take a path cut into the rock on the left: this

Il-Qolla, north of the Chadwick Lakes

walled path on a viaduct leads up to the **Dwejra Lines**. It is not hard to see why the lines were built here, as their commanding position affords magnificent views all over the islands. With their gun emplacements, the lines are a military historian's paradise. The former route along the Lines has become overgrown, so follow instead the track to the right.

Towards the end of the lines, at a FORT COMPLEX, descend between the buildings (**2h20min**). In a few minutes the track turns right then left and meets a minor road coming up from the Mgarr/Mosta road. Turn left here, cross the ditch, and where the road begins to turn right downhill, take a track to the left, parallel with the ditch, for no more than 100m/yds. When the track begins to curve sharply away to the left, turn right and follow a path on the right-hand side of the Lines. Your immediate goal is to pass between the Lines and a FARM BUILDING in about five minutes (**2h45min**). Continue following the Lines: the path

becomes steeper for a time, before you reach the MOSTA/ MGARR ROAD in **2h50min**. (Walk 9 begins about 400m/yds to your left, at the Falka pumping station.)

Cross the busy road, turn left, and in no more than 25m/yds, turn right on a poorly surfaced road, passing a QUARRY on the right. You come upon several small military buildings, some of which are used for farming. At about **3h05min** the walk ends on the MOSTA/ST PAUL'S BAY ROAD, just above **Targa Gap**. At the bus stop (Gharusa) in the direction of Mosta and Valletta a pleasant surprise awaits you — a public garden with striking views to the coast (Picnic 13). Catch the bus back to Mosta Dome (Rotunda stop), which is only 1km/0.6mi distant, or to Valletta; alternatively, at the stop opposite, catch the bus to Bugibba and Mellieha.

Walk 14 MALTA: RABAT (GARGIR) • TAL-LUNZJATA RIDGE • DINGLI • TA' BALDU • TAT-TARGA • RABAT (GARGIR)

See also photographs on pages 22, 23

Distance: 16km/10mi; 3h40min

Grade: easy, with some rocky paths around the coast; overall ascent/descent of 170m/550ft

Equipment: stout shoes, sunhat, waterproofs, water

How to get there and return: 🚌 51, 53 from Valletta to Rabat. Departures every 10-20min; journey time about 40min. The bus does a clockwise circuit of Rabat and will take you to the Gargir bus stop in the Nigred Housing Estate, where the walk begins. Reboard at the stop on the opposite side of the road.

Short walk 1: Busugrilla roundabout — Dingli (6.9km/4.3mi; 1h30min; easy, with an ascent of 90m/300ft and descent of 40m/125ft). Follow the main walk to Dingli and return on 🚌 52.

Short walk 2: Dingli — Dingli Cliffs — Dingli (5.4km/3.4mi; 1h05min; easy, almost level walking). Take 🚌 52 to Dingli and follow the main walk from the village centre to the Coastal Surveillance Post (15min). About 1.5km (1mi) further on, turn right on a narrow tarred road, soon passing some large irrigation tanks and a windmill in the lower ground on your left. In another five minutes, when a narrow road joins from the right, continue straight on. The dome of Dingli church is now in sight. A semi-detached house called Carmel/S Gaetano comes up on

your right, as does a final windmill. Five minutes later bear left around the church in Dingli. Continue on to the main Dingli/Rabat road, where there is a shelter for 🚌 52 to the right.

Shorter start to main walk (saves 25min): Alight from 🚌 51, 53 at the Barka stop (two stops before the alighting point for the main walk). Turn left in 50m/yds on a road signposted 'Santa Katerina'. In about five minutes come to a three-way junction at a house called Madonnina. Bear left here, to Santa Rita, a building where the main walk arrives from the lane on your right. Pick up the main walk at the 30min-point.

Alternative walk: Dingli — Ta' Baldu — Mtahleb — Rabat (Busugrilla) (11.5km/7.2mi; 3h10min; grade as main walk, with an ascent of 90m/300ft and descent of 130m/425ft). Take 🚌 52 to Dingli and follow the main walk from Dingli village centre to Ta' Baldu (1h20min). On leaving the hamlet, turn left on a cliff-top path (by some cart ruts). Follow this path to a pig farm, where you keep the first building on your right. Meeting a road a minute later, bear left and follow a track to Mtahleb church. From the church take some steps on your left down to another road, by the 'CoRRS' (Centre of Residential Restorative Services; formerly Mtahleb School). Turn right and use the map to return to Rabat.

M alta's remote western coastal region, bounded by high vertical cliffs, is the setting for this delightful walk. The ramble also takes in the picturesque hamlet of Santa Katerina set in tranquil countryside.

Old farmhouse on the outskirts of Rabat, possibly dating from 1760

Start off at the GARGIR BUS STOP in the Nigred Housing Estate in **Rabat**: Bear left along TRIQ GĦAJN KAZZET. Turn left on the second of two lanes (**5min**) — just 100m/yds after passing to the left of the old farmhouse shown above, with a coat of arms dated 1760. This lane, which has a 'STOP' sign and a mirror to assist drivers with oncoming traffic at the junction, leads uphill to a small hamlet, passing a large farm in one minute. On reaching **Salvatur** (**9min**), turn left at a farm building (there is a disused wind-pump on the left). A minute later, turn right, and soon go left at a house called ID-DULLURI. *(There have been chained dogs on the left-hand side of the road here in the past; at press date an aggressive dog was housed in a cage.)* In another minute you come to a T-JUNCTION, WHERE THERE IS A DOOR IN A WALL. Turn right here: the small road swings round to the left at yet another farm (QAMMA FARM) and you reach **Tat-Targa Gap** (**16min**).

82

Turn left on a very narrow road. You may wish to pause for a moment to savour the view of the Fiddien (Silvery) Plain. Ignore the road downhill through the gap — it will be your return route. Continue south along **Tal-Lunzjata Ridge** past the CHURCH and convent complex, with its hermitage farmhouse and UNDERGROUND CHAPEL (**20min**). Follow the road round to the left. In two minutes continue straight on, ignoring a track to the right. A minute later ignore a small road on your left. After passing a QUARRY entrance, follow the quiet lane uphill; there are GREENHOUSES on your right and the Ghar Barka Housing Estate on the outskirts of Rabat lies beyond the fields on your left. Soon, take a very narrow lane on your right (it is only 30m/yds long). Turn right at a farmhouse incorporating a shrine on a wall (**30min**).

(The 'Shorter start' joins the main walk here.)
Follow this road downhill through pleasant farmland and descend into the picture-postcard hamlet of **Santa Katerina**, with its incredible church clinging to the hillside and an ancient farmhouse built into the side of the cliffs. Avoid the sharp S-bend by turning left immediately after passing the church; then, after 30m/yds, next to a new house, go down a

flight of steps. At **45min**, just before a SPRING and a farm on the hillside, turn left along a sandy cart track which winds through an area of intensive farming. The spring flowers add splodges of yellow and, occasionally, blue to the canvas along the roadside and on the terraced walls. Keep bearing right, climbing up past a WELL.

When you come to a fork, where the left-hand turning has a 'private' sign (**55min**), carry straight on. In three minutes you reach an old farm building close to the edge of Dingli. Bear left around this building and, almost immediately, go straight ahead (by another WELL). In a further two minutes turn left at a little garden (IL-GARDIN TAX-XAGHRA) onto TRIQ CLAUDETTE AGIUS (1975-1990), at a house called BLANZUNI (**1h05min**). At the end

The Dingli Cliffs, with Il-Kullana (The Necklace) in the background

of the street, take some steps between garages, turn left and, a minute later, turn right into TRIQ SALVU AZZOPARDI (1902-1976). In 80m/yds turn left on TRIQ SAN PAWL to the church. From here go left down TRIQ IL-PARROCCA to the main road. You have arrived at the commercial centre of **Dingli** (**1h10min**), where there are shops, a bank, the club/bar of Dingli Swallows Football Club, and a BUS STOP.

Turn right and follow the main road (TRIQ IL-KBIRA) towards the Dingli Cliffs. At DINGLI CEMETERY bear right: the edge of the **Dingli Cliffs** is reached at a COASTAL SURVEILLANCE POST (**1h25min**). Turn right now, and a house called RIDUM DEPIRO on the left (**1h35min**) should provide your next landmark. Carry on along the cliff-edge. The road, which has become a roughly-tarred track at this point, ends at the PULVICH EXPLOSIVES INDUSTRIES factory on your right (**1h55min**). Proceed down a path to the left of the factory entrance gate, to meet a track in about five minutes. Turn right, and in no more than 15m/ yds join a narrow road coming from the direction of Dingli. Turn left towards the coast and in five minutes (**2h05min**) arrive at a SMALL FARM. I would recommend a detour from here to the end of the road where there are fine views of the coast and the wide valley of the Wied ir-Rum and beyond, towards three oddly shaped hillocks. You should allow about 15-20 minutes for this diversion.

The main walk turns right at the farm — where you should ask for permission, telling him you want to walk to Ta'Baldu. *And beware of the three chained dogs on both sides of the lane (it is best to walk in the middle of the lane, as the dogs are on short chains).* The trail descends via hairpin bends into the **Wied ir-Rum**. If you look back, you'll see the farm has been housed in a complex of Bronze Age caves on the edge of the cliff.

It's a steep climb up the far side to the ridge at **Ta' Baldu**, where you encounter a crossroads (**2h30min**). Turn left here, skirt TA' BALDU HOUSE, and then take the old walled cart track. There are fine views to the south, where walled terraces snuggle up to the well-tended orchards. Soon a surfaced road comes underfoot (**2h50min**).

Now we visit ancient Malta, by following this narrow road downhill into a huddle of small buildings perched on the cliff-edge. Sheep and an occasional shepherd are likely to be your only companions here. On leaving the hamlet, follow the road (little more than a track) around to the right and turn right at a T-junction (**3h05min**). Then turn left in a further ten minutes and go straight ahead two minutes later, past a FARMHOUSE on the right and a vineyard called FRA BRETTEL ESTATE on your left. You are crossing the floor of the plain, and the gap in the cliff-face is your target. This is the road you should have noted in the early part of the walk.

At just under **3h20min** you should be climbing up through **Tat-Targa Gap**. Turning left at the gap, you are now on the road taken earlier. Retrace your steps to the T-junction with the DOOR IN THE WALL on your right. Go straight ahead. At this point Mdina's cathedral is visible on the horizon. You meet the main road at the NIGRED HOUSING ESTATE (**3h40min**): turn right to the BUS STOP.

Walk 15 MALTA: RABAT (FERRIS) • WIED TA' L-ISQOF • GNIEN IL-KBIR • RABAT (DUMNIKANI)

See map pages 88-89; see also Walk 3

Distance: 4km/2.5mi; 55min

Grade: easy, with an overall ascent/descent of 60m/200ft

Equipment: stout shoes, sunhat, waterproofs, picnic, water

How to get there: 🚌 51, 52, 53 from Valletta to Rabat (departures every 10min; journey time 40min); stay on the bus at Rabat interchange as it will continue to its destination. Alight at the junction of Triq Tal-Virtu and Triq Gorg Borg Olivier in Rabat (Ferris bus stop).

To return: 🚌 51, 52, 53 at Dumnikani bus stop opposite the Dominican Monastery to Valletta

Alternative walk 1: Rabat (Tal-Virtu) — Wied ta' l-Isqof — Siggiewi (5.8km/3.6mi; 1h05min; easy, with a descent of 85m/275ft). This is a very pleasant walk on a summer's evening, when the Rabat/Siggiewi road is quiet and the low sun highlights the terraced fields and distant villages. Follow the main walk to the *wied* (21min), then go straight on to the Rabat/Siggiewi road. Follow this to the right. Pass the San Blas chapel (30min) and, ten minutes later, at a complex junction, take the second exit on your left. Bear right at a small stone building (*ignore* the left fork here, signposted to Siggiewi). Pass a memorial (55min) and ignore a small road on the left to Siggiewi. On reaching the outskirts of Siggiewi (1h), bear left (signposted Siggiewi Centre) into Triq Lapsi. In two minutes, where the street narrows, go straight ahead into Triq il-Knisha l-Qadima, to reach the square (photograph page 99) and bus stop.

Alternative walk 2: Rabat (Tal-Virtu) — Wied ta' l-Isqof — Verdala Palace (4.8km/3mi; 1h; easy, with an ascent of 100m/325ft and a descent of 85m/275ft). Follow Alternative walk 1 to the San Blas chapel. Turn right and in five minutes (35min) Walk 16 comes in from your left. Pick up that walk at the 1h30min-point (see page 91).

It is often said that Malta remains a deeply religious country, and this little ramble takes you past the Apostolic Nunciature, the Archbishop's Seminary, a convent, an ancient church and — near the end of the walk — the impressive Dominican Church and Monastery, with cloisters dating from the early 17th century. This walk also reveals just how undulating the landscape can be; the walk descends very steeply but, happily, the climb back up to Rabat via the Wied ta' l-Isqof is long and gradual.

The walk begins at TRIQ TAL-VIRTU in **Rabat**: stroll along this quiet suburban street. Opposite the **Apostolic Nunciature** there is a spectacular viewpoint over the surrounding countryside (**5min**; Picnic 15). The next landmark comes up a minute later: the **Archbishop's Seminary** and the **Convent of the Sacred Heart**. In a further three minutes, bear right around the high wall enclosing **Tal-Virtu** CHURCH and a fairy-tale CASTLE (**9min**). The tranquil gardens are not open to the public.

This lovely shrine at the 34min-point is an important landmark on this walk: it alerts you to a right turn which you might otherwise miss in a landscape devoid of strong features.

The views at this point are now towards the settings for Walk 16 — Verdala Palace, with Laferla Cross visible in the distance. Soon the way becomes a narrow road that plunges down the hillside, so engage low gear. On the higher terraces, there are vineyards and fruit trees; further on, prickly pear 'hedges' and larger trees line the route. Then, on lower ground, the landscape opens out into quite large fields (by Maltese standards). Go straight on past a group of FARM BUILDINGS (**20min**) but, just one minute later, turn right on a small road leading up the **Wied ta' l-Isqof** (there are two small buildings at this junction).

Your route is sandwiched between thick bamboo, which lines the watercourse, and high field walls. Ignore all side tracks left and right. Some 14 minutes along (**34min**) pass a small SHRINE set into a wall at the right and almost immediately after turn right. You come to a group of farm buildings. Take the right-hand fork here, which then twists left before heading uphill and passing two garages on the left at around the **37min**-point. Where the track ends, go up a short ramp and follow a foot-path that rises to the perimeter wall at the rear of the Archbishop's Seminary, where you bear right. The path skirts the wall, first in an easterly direction, then turns sharply left and squeezes into a narrow gap between two walls before emerging on the outward route of the walk (**45min**).

Turn left and retrace your steps back to the start of the walk (**52min**). At the junction of TRIQ TAL-VIRTU and TRIQ GORG BORG OLIVIER turn left: in three minutes (**55min**) you will reach the baroque church of **Madonna tal-Ghar** (Our Lady of the Grotto) and the **Dominican Monastery**. There are bus stops here (Dumnikani) in the direction of Mtarfa/Dingli/Wied iz-Zurrieq and on the opposite side of the road for Rabat interchange/Valletta. Walk 3 begins at the Pjazza Saqqaja a few bus stops away in Rabat — and there's no reason why you shouldn't easily combine the two.

Walk 16 MALTA: BUSKETT • GHAR IL-KBIR • LAFERLA CROSS • VERDALA PALACE

See also photograph page 92
Distance: 8.2km/5.1mi; 1h55min
Grade: easy, with some rougher walking up to the cave at Ghar il-Kbir. Ascent of 140m/450ft; descent of 115m/375ft
Equipment: stout shoes, sunhat, waterproofs, picnic, water
How to get there: 🚌 56 from Valletta to Buskett via Rabat and Dingli. Departures every hour; journey time 1h15min.
To return: 🚌 56 to Valletta or 🚌 181 to Mater Dei Hospital; change buses at Rabat inter-change for other destinations.
Short walk 1: Buskett Gardens. Several well-established walkways in the gardens offer short, easy walks (Picnic 16).
Short walk 2: Buskett — Wied il-Luq — Verdala Palace (5.8km/ 3.6mi; 1h20min; easy; ascent of 100m/325ft and descent of 75m/ 250ft). Follow the main walk for 33min (just past the small quarry), then turn left on the small road leading to the Girgenti Valley.

Follow this down to a bridge over the *wied*, then pick up the main walk again at the 1h15min-point and follow it to the end.

88

T his is one of Malta's loveliest walks, with something of interest for every rambler. We cover ground more familiar to local people than tourists and visit palaces and cave dwellings ... as well as Malta's 'Clapham Junction' (named after London's frenetically busy railway station).

Setting out from the government's OENOLOGY AND VITICULTURE RESEARCH STATION, where the bus stops, in 100m/yds turn right (south) and then left very soon afterwards (signposted GHAR IL-KBIR/CLAPHAM JUNCTION). In **6min** turn right to a CAR PARK. From the car park follow a track for about a minute, to the point where it bends to the left at a field wall. Now a path leads up to a large fallen-in cave (**Ghar il-Kbir; 12min**). Believe it or not, the cave was inhabited until 1835! Close by is 'Clapham Junction' — the name British visitors have given to the large number of prehistoric cart-ruts found in this area.

But back to the cave: retrace

your steps to the car park (**20min**) and turn right downhill on a track. When you approach a wall and gate in two minutes, turn right 15m/yds before the gate (there are some cart ruts here). After 60m/yds pass a shooter's hut and after another 100m/yds, a TELEGRAPH POLE. Some 50m/yds further on, go left, through a GAP IN THE WALL (**25min**). Follow a path which bends left and, in about three minutes, scramble down to a lower level, closer to a *wied*. In another two minutes skirt round a short stretch of modern wall that extends from the gates of the TA' ZUTA QUARRY No 35 towards the *wied* (**30min**). (A water outlet from the quarry

The cart-ruts at Ghar il-Kbir. These strange formations occur on many plateau areas on Malta and have puzzled archaeologists, who believe they date from the Bronze Age. In some places, cart-tracks of several different gauges converge.

here.) The road contours round the hill and then turns left to **St Lawrence Chapel (50min)**. From here turn left along a walled-in path; in a further five minutes you reach **Laferla Cross** and the **Annunciation Chapel**. On the summit a spectacular view greets you — a bird's-eye view of the more urban face of Malta.

The track downhill is lined with statues; it meets the SIGGIEWI ROAD at **1h05min**. Turn left on the road and then left again almost immediately. In about five minutes the road swings left at a STONE PILLAR (inscribed GR). Take the track to the right here, passing a FARMHOUSE in a minute. The track deteriorates into a path running between stone walls before improving to a concrete surface. You cross the **Wied il-Luq** on a narrow BRIDGE (**1h15min**), then cross a track, and after 60m/yds cross a road *(Short walk 16-2 comes in from the left here)*. Go straight ahead up a narrow road flanked by small farm buildings. In 15 minutes (**1h30min**) turn left on another road *(where Alternative walk 15-2 comes in from the right)*. After a further 15 minutes of steady climbing, Verdala Palace emerges from the woodland like a French château. Begun in 1586, it was designed as a safe summer retreat for the Grand Master de Verdalle. Once at the boundary wall of **Verdala Palace (1h50min)**, bear right to the RABAT/BUSKETT ROAD (**1h55min**). The BUS SHELTER (Verdala) is 50m/yds to the left.

may make the going wet for a few metres just before the wall.) Do not pause at the quarry gates or staff car park on working days; there is much heavy traffic, and if you need to check your notes, I suggest you do this at the nearby Mundu bus stop. (At this point you could detour left for 500m/yds, to a viewpoint over the Girgenti Valley and the Inquisitor's Palace, a summer residence built by Inquisitor Onorati Visconti in the 17th century.)

Follow the road uphill to the right for about two minutes, then go left in front of another QUARRY. A minute later (**33min**), turn right on a narrow country road. *(Short Walk 2 goes left*

Walk 17 MALTA: TA' ZUTA • RDUM DIKKIENA • GHAR LAPSI • HAGAR QIM • WIED IZ-ZURRIEQ

Map begins on pages 88-89
Distance: 11.5km/7.2mi; 2h55min
Grade: moderate; an ascent of 170m/550ft and descent of 365m/1200ft
Equipment: stout shoes, sunhat, swimwear, waterproofs, picnic, water
How to get there: 🚌 201 from Rabat to Ta' Zuta (departures every hour); journey time 17min.
To return: 🚌 201 to Rabat (hourly), or 🚌 74 to Valletta.
Short walk: Buskett — Ghar Lapsi (6.4km/4mi; 1h35min; fairly easy). End the walk at Ghar Lapsi to avoid the climb; pre-arrange a taxi pick-up at the Lapsi Restaurant.

Alternative walk: Buskett — Ghar Lapsi — Hagar Qim — Qrendi (11.2km/7.0mi; 2h50min; moderate; an ascent of 180m/600ft and descent of 245m/800ft). Follow the main walk to the Hagar Qim temples, then walk on to the main road. Take the road almost opposite towards Qrendi. On approaching the village, bear right into Misrah Il-Maqluba, to visit the collapsed limestone depression known as Il-Maqluba, adjacent to a chapel dedicated to St Matthew. Follow Triq San Matthew towards the village centre; the 🚌 72 terminus for Valletta is in front of the church.

T his walk includes several of Malta's most popular tourist attractions, the prehistoric temples at Hagar Qim and Mnajdra, and the spectacular coastal scenery at the Blue Grotto. It also provides a rare opportunity to visit an under-cliff area.

The walk starts at the ZUTA BUS STOP on the Dingli Cliffs. Turn onto a rocky trail which heads straight for the vertical cliff-edge. Five minutes along, you come to the end of a promontory known as **Il-Wardija ta' San Gorg**. Look carefully for signs of the NEOLITHIC SETTLEMENT here, including some bell-shaped underground excavations used for the storage of cereals. This area is also home to the national plant, the *Centaurea crassifolia* (Widnet il-Bahar or Malta knapweed). The track descends in a series of sharp hairpin bends, where the coastal scenery provides a feast for the senses.

At **15min Tal-Karmnu Chapel**, with a fine belvedere, appears. A man-made cave, complete with stone furniture, lies in the small garden below it. Continuing on, the narrow road passes two farmhouses, one of which was owned by Sir Basil Spence, the architect of Coventry Cathedral. **Tal-Lunzjata Chapel** comes up at about **25min**. After passing two converted farmhouses on your left (**35min, 40min**), continue straight ahead downhill until the SIGGIEWI/GHAR LAPSI road is reached (**50min**).

Turn right, passing ID-DAR TAL-PROVIDENZA, a home for the disabled, on your right. Reach a roundabout, follow signs for Ghar Lapsi, and in a further two minutes pass a QUARRY on your right. Under two minutes later, a sharp hairpin bend (**1h05min**) signals the start of the descent to

Verdala Palace and Buskett Gardens (Picnic 16). The high walls once enclosed a deer park.

Ghar Lapsi. Although there is a water purification plant at **Ghar Lapsi** (**1h20min**; Picnic 17a), there is a lovely cove by the restaurant, where you can swim and picnic.

So far the walk has been all downhill, but now comes the hard part! Your waymarkers are the two WATER PIPELINES up the cliff. Go back to these water pipes and take a track on the right to the foot of a hill. Cross to the opposite side and proceed uphill on a path. Towards the top of the steepest section look for rough-hewn steps on the left: take these to the HAGAR QIM/ ZURRIEQ ROAD opposite a building with blue shutters — by which time you will have climbed 115m/375ft (**1h40min**).

Turn right on the road and after passing a QUARRY on the right (**1h50min**), turn right on a track by a gate and descend to the floor of an abandoned QUARRY that has now become a NATURE AREA with waymarked trails. In a further two minutes, on rounding a corner in the quarry face (on top of which there is a building), *don't* be tempted to take the path that leads uphill to the left. Instead, continue straight on, passing some old quarry building foundations. A watchtower soon comes into view on the horizon.

From here a rough track takes you downhill to the temples at **Mnajdra** (**2h**). The temples are close to the cliff-edge and are protected by a high fence. It is recommended that you approach the temples via a track from the left (landward) side of the site. From Mnajdra take the paved walkway to the temples of **Hagar Qim (2h05min)**, where you should skirt these temples on the right (seaward) side to reach a modern building that houses a bar/restaurant and visitor centre.

From here the easiest way to get to the famous Blue Grotto is to turn right on the main Zurrieq road, just a minute away. (For those of you with a strong aversion to walking on roads, it is possible to catch Bus 201 to Wied iz-Zurrieq from Hagar bus stop on the main road opposite the entrance to Hagar Qim.)

Continuing along the road, you reach the picture-postcard hamlet at the mouth of the **Wied iz-Zurrieq** (Picnic 17b) in **2h40min**. Amongst the colourful boats and boathouses there are boatmen ready to ferry you into the **Blue Grotto** if the sea is calm.

The Blue Grotto — one of Malta's most popular attractions

From the hamlet walk back up to the CAR PARK (**2h45min**) and catch Bus 201 there or, alternatively, another 10 minutes of tiring uphill walking will bring you to the MAIN ROAD (**2h55min**), where you could wait for Bus 74 to Valletta at the Panorama bus stop (100m/yds in the direction of Zurrieq).

Those with energy for more walking can continue on foot to Qrendi for the more frequent Bus 72 to Valletta. For this option, go straight across the main road into a minor road signposted to QRENDI. This leads through pleasant countryside to Misrah Il-Maqluba on the village outskirts. Turn right at a traffic island, where the minor road from Hagar Qim comes in from the left (Alternative walk). Follow TRIQ SAN MATTEW, MISRAH SAN MATTEW and TRIQ IL-PAROCCA to reach the BUS TERMINUS in the *pjazza* in front of Qrendi's CHURCH (3h20min). The terminus and church are shown in the photograph on page 133.

Walk 18 MALTA: SIGGIEWI • TAL-PROVIDENZA • SAN NIKLAW CHAPEL • SIGGIEWI

See map on pages 94-95; see also photograph page 99
Distance: 6.4km/4mi; 1h40min
Grade: very easy, almost level walking
Equipment: stout shoes, sunhat, waterproofs, water
How to get there and return:
🚌 62 from Valletta to Siggiewi (departures every 20min; journey time 40min); alight in the main square.
Short walk: Siggiewi — Tal-Providenza — Siggiewi
(3.2km/2mi; 50min; grade as main walk). Follow the main walk for 25min; on reaching Tal-Providenza church, turn left and follow the main walk from the 1h15min-point.

Alternative walk: Siggiewi — Verdala Palace (6.1km/3.8mi; 1h20min; easy, with an ascent of 90m/300ft). Follow the main walk as far as the irrigation tank on the Ghar Lapsi road (14min) and, a minute later, turn right on a narrow asphalt road. Follow this through high stone-walled fields dotted with dozens of small stone storage huts. When you meet the Siggiewi road at a T-junction, turn right. Within two minutes you join the route of Walk 16; use the notes for that walk from the 1h05min-point (page 91) to reach Verdala Palace.

A charming village, richly-farmed countryside, and wayside chapels … everything about this walk conjures up traditional Malta. The bus ride to Siggiewi is fascinating — a windmill, narrow streets lined by old houses with little alleys (known as *sqaq*), and masons crafting ornamental stone in workshops are all to be seen.

Alight at the bus terminus at the lower end of the large L-shaped square (PJAZZA SAN NIKOLA). Pause a moment to soak up the village atmosphere … the

church dedicated to St Nicholas (photograph page 99), the clubhouse of the village band, the 'Friend to All' bar, small chapels, political party clubs

Tal-Providenza church

and, in the centre, a statue of the patron saint (St Nicholas) dating from 1734.

Then **start the walk**: turn right past the St Nicholas statue, into the lower square. Head for a narrow street flanked by the POLICE STATION and an old CHAPEL (**2min**). Several alleys lead from this street (Triq il-Knisja l-Qadima): in ancient times, when pirates and corsairs came ashore to pillage, these could be blocked off easily. At a junction where the streets become much wider (**5min**), continue straight ahead into Triq Lapsi (signposted to Ghar Lapsi). The village outskirts and bypass are reached in another three minutes. Follow SIGNS FOR GHAR LAPSI and go straight ahead, into a road. Tal-Providenza church on the horizon provides an unmistakable landmark, and MARITA FARM HOUSE comes up on your right in **11min**. Two minutes later, at a large irrigation tank, there are fine views back to Siggiewi, while Laferla Cross (Walk 16) and Mdina (Walk 3) can be seen on the right.

At about **25min** leave the road at a GARDEN CENTRE and turn left to **Tal-Providenza** church, with its impressive dome and interesting covered entrance. Turn right along a track, and in two minutes regain the Ghar Lapsi road at two converted farmhouses, Tal-Brimb and Tal-Gholja. No more than two minutes later, at another old WATER TANK which incorporates a MEMORIAL (**30min**), ignore the rather overgrown track on the left. But take the *next* track on the left, 70m/yds further on. This passes a house called La Mirage and twists right and then left, to run parallel with the old Qrendi AIRFIELD (**33min**), where a

runway and hangars were built during World War II to provide additional air support for the Allied invasion of Sicily. Follow its boundary for about 10 minutes, with fine views over intensively-farmed countryside on your left. Towards the end of the airfield (**43min**) the track turns left and, almost immediately, right (ignore the cul-de-sac track to the left).

In **50min** you arrive at the small 18th-century **San Niklaw Chapel**. Turn left here, and *beware of dogs* that sometimes guard buildings on both sides of the road. Tal-Providenza is again your goal, and the narrow road descends into a shallow valley dotted with small buildings. At **1h15min** you should be back at a farm complex about 100m/yds east of Tal-Providenza church. Ignore the turn to the right, and in 50m/yds one to the left that would take you back to the church. Instead go straight ahead to regain your outward route, and when you are almost back at the main road, turn right at a high walled-in enclosure. Two minutes along, turn left into a very narrow road between high walls. Siggiewi church is now in sight. In about 10 minutes you come to the SIGGIEWI/QRENDI ROAD at a roundabout (**1h28min**). Go straight on, following signs for ZEBBUG and MQABBA. In **1h30min**, at another round-about, ignore the 'Siggiewi Centre' sign; go straight on (towards 'ZEBBUG/QORMI'). In 300m/yds, just before a pedestrian crossing, turn left on Triq Nikola Saura. Then follow Triq il-Qajjied into the MAIN SQUARE at **Siggiewi**. The BUS STOP (Is-Siggiewi) for Valletta is on the north side of the square (**1h40min**).

Walk 19 MALTA: SIGGIEWI • WIED IL-HESRI • WIED QIRDA • WIED IL-KBIR • QORMI

See also photograph page 22
Distance: 7.2km/4.5mi; 2h05min
Grade: quite easy, some scrambling and rougher walking in the lower Wied Qirda. *Do not attempt this walk in wet weather.* Descent of 110m/350ft
Equipment: stout shoes, sunhat, waterproofs, water
How to get there: 🚐 62 from Valletta to Siggiewi (departures every 20min; journey time 40min); alight in the main square.
To return: 🚐 62 from Qormi to Valletta
Short walk 1: Siggiewi — Wied il-Hesri — Siggiewi (3.2km/2mi; 50min; easy, with an ascent/descent of 40m/125ft). Follow the main walk and cross the bridge over the Wied il-Hesri. Turn left on a track for about 15 minutes, then leave the valley at the point where a tarmac road leads uphill (near a stone building). This meets a road in a couple of minutes.

Turn left back into the centre of Siggiewi. Return on 🚐 62.
Short walk 2: Siggiewi — Zebbug (2.4km/1.5mi; 40min; easy, with a descent of 50m/175ft). Follow the main walk as far as Hal Mula, on the outskirts of Zebbug, and catch 🚐 62 back to Valletta.

Siggiewi church

Short walk 3: Zebbug — Qormi
(4.8km/3mi; 1h25min; grade as
Short walk 2). Take 62 as for
the main walk, but alight at Hal

Mula on the outskirts of Zebbug.
Follow the main walk from the
40min-point.

L ike Walk 18, this ramble begins at Siggiewi. But this
time your route follows a succession of secluded
valleys. While some are flanked by cultivated fields,
others are so isolated that they have become home to
fireworks factories!

Set off from **Siggiewi** by
following the one-way signs for
traffic leaving the SQUARE,
heading northwest along TRIQ
IL-PARROCCA. Go through a small
square called MISRAH SAN
GWANN, then follow TRIQ
IL-MITHNA. In just under **5min**
you reach a complicated
crossroads at the edge of the
older part of the village. Turn
right along TRIQ WIED IL-HESRI;
Mosta Dome should be visible
on the horizon. Follow this road
to the SIGGIEWI SPORTS COMPLEX
(**6min**) and bear right round the
sports field, heading downhill.
Your way becomes a grassy
track through fields, and you
descend into the **Wied il-Hesri**.
Turn left, cross the BRIDGE and

go right on a narrow tarmac
track, parallel with the stream
(**13min**). Ignore any tracks on
the left which head up the side
of the valley (especially the first
one: it leads to a fireworks
factory; you'll spot warning
signs and a red flag). The next
landmark is a small TOWER. Not
far beyond it, the track crosses
the *wied* and, near a group of
FARM BUILDINGS, it swings left,
away from the *wied* (**25min**).
Don't follow the track up to the
farm, but bear round to the
right, soon returning to the
valley floor. At about **35min** the
narrow *wied* is sandwiched
between an elevated section of
the Siggiewi/Zebbug road and
high terrace walls.

Top: chapel dedicated to the Visitation of St Elizabeth by Our Lady, at Wied Qirda.
Below: even though MPT have replaced Malta's wonderful old buses with new models, this farm truck encountered just before the end of the walk is a fine reminder of days gone by,

opposite, dates from the early 18th century.

Continue past an abandoned farmhouse and another FIRE-WORKS FACTORY. At **55min** the track swings right. The valley becomes narrower and deeper. At **1h05min**, where the main track leads to yet another FIRE-WORKS FACTORY, go straight ahead on another track. After 50m/yds, where this track also swings right, take the path straight ahead; it descends to the dry watercourse in the valley floor. Pick your way along the canyon-like valley, avoiding the large boulders. The path slowly improves to a rough track (**1h40min**), as you leave the narrowest section of the valley.

The **Wied Hanzir** now joins from the right, and the com-bined valley becomes the **Wied il-Kbir**. An orchard has been planted here. Pass a farmhouse on your left, beyond which the surface of the track improves. Working farms, a garage, green-houses, a flower nursery, yet another fireworks factory(!) and rooftop guard dogs are your companions now, until you reach the busy QORMI/LUQA ROAD (**2h**). The dome of modern Qormi church is now in sight. Turn left and in five minutes reach a roundabout on the outskirts of **Qormi**. Turn left into TRIQ L-IMDINA and use the pelican crossing to reach the BUS STOP (Tin) on the far side of the dual carriageway.

At just under **40min** another *wied* and road come in from the left. A bus stop (Qirda) at **Hal Mula**, on the SIGGIEWI/ZEBBUG ROAD, lies ahead. There is a bus shelter here which may be welcome. Otherwise take the path under the ROAD BRIDGE and continue straight on down the valley, which now becomes the **Wied Qirda**. On your left you can just see an embankment that was intended to carry the main road over the valley; the project was abandoned, and a small public garden was laid out instead (now derelict). The next landfall is the 17th-century chapel shown above, dedicated to the **Visitation of St Elizabeth by Our Lady** (**45min**). The building at the rear is a fine example of a fortified farmhouse. Another farmhouse,

Walk 20 MALTA: MARSAXLOKK • WIED HAS-SABTAN • GUDJA

Distance: 8km/5mi; 2h25min
Grade: easy, with an ascent of 130m/425ft and descent of 50m/175ft
Equipment: stout shoes, sunhat, waterproofs, picnic, water

How to get there: 🚌 81 from Valletta to Marsaxlokk. Departures every 20min; journey time about 35-40min
To return: 🚌 88 from Gudja to Valletta

Early societies are a feature of many of the walks in this book, and in the course of this ramble you can visit a Bronze Age village and prehistoric cart ruts.

Begin at **Marsaxlokk** by dodging your way past the quayside stalls; follow the bay southwards until the road splits. Ignore the left fork to Birzebbuga that takes the easy (but less exciting) way along the coast to the Ferretti Battery and Borg in-Nadur. Instead, follow the road that climbs slightly to the right (TRIQ IT-TORRI VERDOME). This leads into TRIQ IL-KAVALLERIZZA (**10min**). Head inland on this street and in 300m/yds pass the charming **Kavallerizza**, shown below. Unfortunately, it's now surrounded by housing development, but is still visible at the end of a short street to the right (**15min**). It was once a riding school for the Knights. Just 100m/yds beyond the

house, turn right. Rise up for just under 1km/0.6mi, to a three-way junction (**30min**), where the main lane bends 90° to the right. Turn left here on the higher of two tracks. (A diversion may be made to the beautiful Palazzo Il-Marnisi by turning right here and continuing for 400 metres/a quarter of a mile.)
In a further five minutes, just after passing an isolated house on the right with a wooden balcony (shown below), you meet a T-junction. *The track to the left is a short-cut, but it passes two scrapyards with nasty, unchained dogs.* So turn right here, to the main BIRZEBBUGA ROAD, where there is a BUS STOP (Marnizi) 50m/yds to

You should be able to recognise the Kavallerizza (opposite), despite the fact that it's now 'lost' in a housing estate. Just 20 minutes later, you pass the isolated house shown below — recently refurbished and with a closed wooden balcony. Until a few years ago, it had wrought-iron balconies. The traditional Maltese closed balcony (gallarija) was always made of wood. Other, low-maintenance materials have been used more recently, but they cannot replicate the traditional design. Now the Maltese government offers grants to promote conservation of the original wooden structures.

the right (**40min**). The road is very busy, and there is no pavement. I strongly recommend that you catch Bus 80 or 82 here and alight at the first stop (Nadur) on the promenade at St George's Bay, a journey of no more than two minutes. On alighting, cross the road and follow the signs to Borg in-Nadur via Triq Alfonso Maria Galea, go right into Sqaq in-Nadur, and take the path up to the defensive wall, which in some places is as high as 5m/15ft. Excavation work carried out here in the 1930s revealed a Bronze Age village site and fortifications, a Copper

ID-DAR TA' PULTU. After no more than 100m/yds, turn right onto a concrete surface which after another 100m/yds becomes a track between terraced fields. In just under five minutes this track ends at a WIRE MESH GATE (**1h25min**). Fork right here, on a path leading out to a stone surface above the **Wied Has-Sabtan**. In another six or seven minutes, when you come to a small stone hut, the path swings to the right, crosses over two pipes and turns left at a higher level.

About **1h50min** should see you at a dilapidated farm, the CASA IPPOLITA, which was built in 1664 by a Sicilian nobleman. Turn *right* on a track which skirts to the east (right) of the farm and climbs gently uphill. In two minutes (**1h52min**) this acquires a concrete surface and in another minute you arrive at a T-junction. Turn left on a narrow road parallel with the *wied,* but some distance away. Pass a farm at at around the **1h55min**-mark come to another T-junction opposite a large red metal farm gate. Turn right uphill, passing FARM VILLE, and five minutes (**2h**) should see you at a magnificent old PILLBOX (Ta Kusinu) and PILLAR. Take a rough track on your left between high dry-stone walls. At a crossroads of sorts (**2h05min**), continue straight ahead on a very narrow road.

On the outskirts of **Gudja**, take TRIQ SAN GORG and TRIQ SAN CIRU to the CHURCH. Turn right here and, almost immediately, go left on TRIQ WILLIAM BAKER. In 250m/yds you reach a public garden and BUS STOP (**2h25min**).

Age temple site and prehistoric cart-ruts.

Retrace your steps to the waterfront and take the road towards Birzebbuga. At the junction two to three minutes later, take the fork furthest to the right (TRIQ BIRZEBBUGA) and, after a few yards/metres, turn right on TRIQ

Walk 21 MALTA: MARSASCALA • ST THOMAS BAY • FORT DELIMARA • MARSAXLOKK

See also photographs on pages 102-103, 108
Distance: 9.9km/6.2mi; 2h30min
Grade: fairly easy, with overall ascent/descent of 110m/350ft
Equipment: stout shoes, sunhat, swimwear, waterproofs, picnic, water
How to get there: 🚍 91, 93 from Valletta to Marsascala (departures every 10min; journey time 35min) or 🚍 124 from Senglea via Zabbar to Marsascala (departures hourly; journey time 25-30min). Alight in the village centre where there are bars and cafes, or stay on the bus until it reaches St Thomas Bay, a saving of 35min.
To return: 🚍 81, 85 from Marsaxlokk to Valletta

View north from Tal-Munxar towards St Thomas Bay and Marsascala

Τhis walk introduces 'Landscapers' to two contrasting communities on the southeast coast. Marsascala has become a fashionable place to live and has a number of cafés and restaurants on its promenade — ideal for a coffee or snack before starting Walk 21 or 22. Marsaxlokk is still a working port, and the brightly coloured boats and quayside market are popular with visitors. Unfortunately the deep waters of Marsaxlokk Bay have also attracted a container terminal and a power station.

Start out in **Marsascala** by walking around Marsascala Bay to the redoubt shown on page 109, the **St Thomas Tower**. Just beyond the (closed) JERMA PALACE HOTEL, you have two options. *In good weather,* cut down to the SALT PANS on the beach and scramble along the rocky foreshore. On coming to a PILLBOX (**25min**), climb up to the low cliff jutting into St Thomas Bay, where you will arrive at a PUBLIC GARDEN (Picnic 21a; **35min**). *In wet weather,* it's best to take roads to the garden: take TRIQ IR-RIDOTT which becomes TRIQ THOMAS ASHBY, turn right into TRIQ PHILIPPE DE VENDOME,

and then go left on a wide road (TRIQ IL-QALIET) to the PUBLIC GARDEN (**35min**).
Walk to the far end of the garden, where a restaurant overlooks **St Thomas Bay**. Carry on along the shore, passing holiday homes, to the far end. At a farm building (**43min**) take the left-hand fork to the point at **Il-Munxar**, which is reached at about the **55min**-mark. Enjoy the dramatic coastal scenery, including a small cliff arch, before tackling the gradual ascent along the cliff path *(keep a safe distance from the edge)* overlooking the neighbouring **Xrobb l-Ghajin** peninsula.

Low cliffs on the outskirts of Marsascala

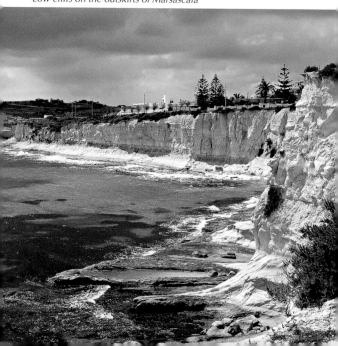

After around seven minutes' walking, when you meet a track, turn left. In another three minutes you pass the small **St Paul Chapel** (**1h**).

Some 200m/yds beyond the chapel, join a narrow road that comes in from the **Xrobb il-Ghagin Peninsula**. In five minutes (**1h10min**), after passing some bushes, go left on a track (at a single leaning tree, where the narrow road turns sharply to the right). After 30m/yds this track swings to the right. Follow it for just two minutes, to a small FARM BUILDING. Descend a few yards/metres as you pass this building. Your way is straight ahead on a terraced shelf between a field wall on your right and a cultivated terrace some 6 feet/2m below. Continue along the edge of terraced fields until you meet a track coming from the right (**1h17min**).

Coastal erosion affecting the cliffs beyond this point means that for safety reasons an inland route is followed. Take the track and, in two minutes, reach a minor road running from Marsaxlokk to Delimara Point. Turn left here to visit **Fort Delimara** (**1h35min**), built by the British in 1881; It's an impressive stronghold with a deep ditch, but is not open to the public. There are fine views from the entrance towards the container port at Kalafrana. From the fort entrance, retrace your steps and follow the ridge road, passing the POWER STATION (**1h55min**) and, on the opposite side of the road, a new house (which was under construction at press date). Keep to this quiet road as far as **Tas-Silg Battery** (**2h15min**) and, from there, take a track on the left down to the ACCESS ROAD for the power station. Turn right and in 50m/yds turn left on a road to colourful **Marsaxlokk** (**2h35min**), Malta's largest fishing village. Visit the open-air market, before boarding your bus in the main street.

Ditch at Fort Delimara and view to the container terminal at Kalafrana

Walk 22 MALTA: MARSASCALA • ZONQOR POINT • XGHAJRA • MARSASCALA

Distance: 9.1km/5.7mi; 2h10min

Grade: easy, with an ascent of 220m/350ft and descent of 90m/300ft

Equipment: stout shoes, sunhat, waterproofs, water, picnic

How to get there and return: 🚌 91, 93 from Valletta to Marsascala (departures every 10min; journey time 35min) or 🚌 124 from Senglea via Zabbar to Marsascala (departures hourly; journey time 25-30min). Alight at Marsascala church. Return using the same bus services, as described on page 110.

Short walk 1: Marsascala — Zonqor Point — Blata l–Bajda — Xghajra (5km/3.1mi; 1h30min; easy, with an ascent/descent of 50m/175ft). Follow the main walk as far as the pillbox (50min), cut down to the coastal path, and turn left to Xghajra's church. Return from there on 🚌 94 to Valletta.

Short walk 2: Xghajra — Blata l–Bajda — Marsascala (3.5km/2.2mi; 1h05min; easy, with an ascent of 45m/150ft and descent of 30m/100ft). Take 🚌 94 from Valletta to the bus stop at Xghajra church on Triq il-Knisja. Follow the main walk from there to Marsascala.

T his is a walk of contrasts: the ridge provides easy walking, with fine views and some architectural curiosities, while the coastal stretch closely hugs the sea, weaving its way among coves and promontories, from watchtowers to forts.

Begin the walk at **Marsascala** church: head off around the north side of the pretty bay. It is possible to pass in front of the houses at the water's edge during the first part of the walk. **Zonqor Point** (**18min**) is your

next landmark, with views across the bay to St Thomas Tower. From here retrace your steps for about three minutes, then turn right uphill on TRIQ IL-BLAJJIET. Turn right again along TRIQ GHAXQET I-GHAJN (**30min**).

This walk begins at Marsascala's church, with its prominent tower; Walk 21 begins on this walkway on the south side of the bay.

Follow this around until it rejoins TRIQ IL-BLAJJIET, where you turn right downhill. After 100m/yds take a narrow, roughly surfaced road on the right (**40min**). This passes a farm, then swings round to the left and becomes wider. The going is easy from now on, affording pleasant walking and good views of the valley to the west. You pass by the lovely little CHAPEL shown overleaf (**45min**; it dates from 1761). A large World War II PILLBOX is your next landmark less than five minutes later (**47min**). *(Short walk 1 cuts down to the coastal path here.)* Soon **Fort San Leonardo** is visible on your right, dating from the late 19th century but now much neglected and used for agricultural purposes. Shortly after passsing PETITA FARM (**57min**), the road swings round to the right. On the next

bend, you come to the ruins of an old house incorporating a chapel. Another ten minutes brings you to the TAL-MILORD CONCRETE READY MIX works, on your left close to a farm. Just before reaching the roundabout on the outskirts of Xghajra (just over **1h10min**), a short stretch of old country lane (SQAQ SAN LEONARDO) can be seen beside a farmhouse. Turn right at the roundabout, and in a few minutes bear left on TRIQ ORLANDO ZABBAR (with a 'no entry' sign). This pedestrianised street leads into TRIQ IL-KNISJA and the centre of **Xghajra**, a re-sort frequented by the Maltese. Make for the coast with its skyline of many watchtowers, and turn back southeast towards Marsascala on a promenade. Just past Xghajra, the San Leonardo Fort, high on the horizon on the right, overlooks the walk. Continue along the

This 18th-century chapel is passed 45min into the walk.

promenade to the salt pans at **Blata l-Bajda** — the next landmark (Picnic 22).

The little bay of **Gorf l-Abjad** (The White Gulf) comes up at the **1h45min**-mark, by which time your route has become a rough track. Ten minutes later, by a small inlet where there are two PILLBOXES and a WATCHTOWER, climb up right, to a track. Follow the track steeply uphill for five minutes, to regain the ridge road (**2h**) by the large PILLBOX encountered on the outward journey.

Walk straight ahead downhill on a narrow road through terraced fields. In under ten minutes you reach the MARSASCALA-ZABBAR ROAD (**2h10min**), where you should catch the bus (Gharghar stop) in either the direction of Marsascala or Senglea and Valletta.

St Thomas Tower (visited on Walk 21)

Walk 23 GOZO: VICTORIA • ZEBBUG • XWIENI BAY • WIED IL-MIELAH • GHARB

Distance: 13km/8.1mi; 2h50min

Grade: easy

Equipment: stout shoes, sunhat, waterproofs, water, picnic

How to get there and return: 🚂 from Malta to Mgarr Harbour, then 🚌 301 from Mgarr to Victoria; journey time 15min

Short walk: Ghasri — Wied il-Ghasri — Gordan Lighthouse — Ghasri (4.2km/2.6mi; 55min; easy, with an ascent/descent of 115m/370ft. From the square in Ghasri (Pjazza Salvatur) fork left along Triq Salvu Gambin and in one minute turn left into Triq il-Knisja. In about 10 minutes pass a stone cross and Tal-Patrocinju church, the oldest on Gozo. Turn left along Triq il-Gonna. In about three minutes, where a road (Triq il-Fanal) comes in from the left, turn right and follow this to Gordan Lighthouse (30min). The return route is straight along Triq il-Fanal to the Ghammar/Ghasri road, where you turn left.

Shorter walk 1: Victoria — Ghasri — Victoria (11.2km/7mi; 3h; easy, with an ascent/descent of 30m/100ft). Follow the main walk to the Wied il-Ghasri, but then turn left up the rough track, to the village of Ghasri, from where you can return to Victoria by Bus 308.

Shorter walk 2: Victoria — Zebbug — Wied il-Ghasri — Xwieni Bay — Marsalforn (8.5km/5.3mi; 2h55min; easy ascent of 30m/100ft and descent of 140m/450ft). Follow the main walk to Zebbug. Bear left at the church, along Triq il-Knisja and Triq il-Madonna ta' Cicri, then turn left on Triq Caqra (Picnic 23a is three minutes straight on, via Triq L-Onici). Continue downhill on a track for 10 minutes, then go straight ahead at a crossroads (by a converted farmhouse). One minute later, when the track swings round to the right, follow it towards the coast and rejoin the main walk at the 2h05min-point. Now use the map to walk to Xwieni Bay and Marsalforn (the main walk in reverse). Return to Victoria on 🚌 310 or to Mgarr on 🚌 322.

Shorter walk 3: Victoria — Zebbug Cemetery — Marsalforn (5.4km/3.4mi; 1h15min; easy, with an ascent/descent of 30m/100ft). Follow the main walk to the larger of the cemeteries (35min). Turn right, passing bus stops (Bez) in both directions, and then left on a narrow road. Ignore all side roads, and after 10 minutes take the right fork which climbs away from the valley floor (the left fork following the Wied il-Qlejgha leads only to a farm). Continue straight ahead on reaching the outskirts of Marsalforn and after passing through an area of apartment blocks, the bus terminus for services to Victoria (310) and Mgarr (322) is reached in another 10 minutes.

A pleasant stroll through a patchwork of fields links Victoria with the large hilltop village of Zebbug. A steep descent then takes us to the coastal salt pans. Then we cross a long stretch of coastal terrain, before returning to village life at Gharb.

Start off in **Victoria**: turn right outside the bus station and walk straight across the crossroads, to join the MARSALFORN ROAD. In **3min** bear left at the GOZO GARAGE, round the base of the CITADEL, and in **10min** come to a 4-WAY JUNCTION. Take the left fork by the restaurant (TRIQ WIED SARA), ignoring the more direct route to Zebbug on your right. Follow this quiet, narrow road towards Ghasri. You cross the **Sara Valley** and wind through tiny green fields interrupted by tabletop hills. Ghasri church comes into view after ten minutes (**20min**). Five minutes later, on reaching the outskirts of **Ghasri**, turn right (**25min**). You pass a small CEMETERY four minutes later and come to a much larger CEMETERY at about the **35min**-mark. *(Shorter walk 3*

112

turns right here.) Bear left here, shortly afterwards beginning the climb to **Zebbug**, a delightful hilltop village. Take the street to the right of the church and follow it to the far end of the village, from where the road descends to the coast via hairpin bends. Spectacular views over the salt pans and the strange coastal rock formations, reminiscent of Neapolitan ice cream, accompany you on this steep descent.

Xwieni Bay (Picnic 23b) is reached at about **1h30min**; its name derives from the galley-shaped rock that dominates it. Turn left around the bay, along an undulating concrete road

that acquires a tarmac surface after 15 minutes. At about **1h55min** turn right on another narrow tarmac road which leads into a shallow little valley. The road soon peters out into a rough track. Where it ends, bear left and follow a path parallel with the **Wied il-Ghasri** for a few minutes. The path gradually improves to a track. Observe a farm on the opposite side of the *wied*; some 150m/yds after passing the farm, the *wied* becomes shallow (**2h05min**). *(Shorter walk 1 turns left here; Shorter walk 2 rejoins the main walk here.)*

Cross over to the other side and turn right, passing the afore-mentioned farm. Ignore the narrow track on the left immediately after the farm; soon your track runs parallel with the cliffs (**2h10min**). Gordan lighthouse stands on the hill to your left. When you reach the **Wied il-Mielah** (**2h25min**), another road comes in (from Gharb.) At the entrance to this w*ied* there is a spectacular arch in the sea cliffs (add five minutes if you detour to the cliffs, and keep a safe distance from the edge).

The walking route now follows the recently improved road next to the stream course inland. In about 10 minutes (**2h35min**) fork left at a small TOWER building and pass several small DAMS. When the road swings

uphill to the right in another five minutes, there are fine views towards Ta'Pinu just before you enter **Gharb**. Traditional houses line the streets, and a small bar and courtyard restaurant will be a welcome sight for those in need of refreshment.

The centre of Gharb is the pleasant PJAZZA TAZ-TJARA TAL-MADONNA which is reached at about **2h50min**. Pause for a moment by the police station to admire the church and fine market cross; there is a folk museum here as well. The hourly bus service (312) to Victoria passes through the *pjazza;* there is also a stop (Punent) for Bus 311 between Victoria and Dwejra five minutes away on the main road.

Below: Xwieni Bay and saltpans; right: Forna Point

Walk 24 GOZO: VICTORIA • XLENDI • KERCEM • DWEJRA BAY • SANTA LUCIJA

See also photographs on pages 25 and 26
Distance: 14km/8.8mi; 4h30min
Grade: easy; overall ascent/descent of 270m/875ft
Equipment: stout shoes, sunhat, swimwear, waterproofs, picnic, water
How to get there: as Walk 23, page 111
To return: 🚌 313 from Santa Lucija to Victoria
Short walk: Victoria — Xlendi (4.5km/2.8mi; 1h; easy, with an ascent/descent of 45m/175ft).

Follow the main walk to Xlendi and return to Victoria on Bus 306 or 330.

Alternative walk: Santa Lucija — Dwejra Bay — Santa Lucija (8.6mi/5.4mi; 3h20min; easy, with an ascent/descent of 160m/525ft). Take Bus 313 to Santa Lucija. At the church turn left into Triq Klula. After 10 minutes you meet another road: turn right and pick up the notes for the main walk at the 1h35min-point.

T his walk visits the fishing village of Xlendi — probably Gozo's favourite attraction, as well as Fungus Rock and the Inland Sea — the island's most spectacular coastal rock formations.

Start out at the BUS STATION in **Victoria:** turn left and follow SIGNPOSTING TO XLENDI. In **5min** continue straight on for Munxar (where the road forks right to Xlendi). Turn right into the outskirts of **Munxar** at **20min** and pass the CHURCH and square. Fork left on TRIQ DUN SPIR GAUCI and climb in a southerly direction. In two

minutes (**22min**) turn right and then immediately left, into TRIQ ZGHAWRI (also signposted to the Sanap Cliffs).
Strike off right again in **30min**, ignoring a road on your left which leads to the Sanap Cliffs (the detour to the viewpoint and a stroll along the scenic cliff walkway takes about 20 minutes return). Follow the road

Approaching Xlendi Bay

parallel with the coast (but some distance inland). In **40min**, at the second of two turn-offs that follow each other in rapid succession, turn left on a track which soon turns into a path. It runs into the river bed, which is flanked by stone walls, and then heads straight for the cliffs. Just before a ruined building, bear left again and, at **50min**, turn right over a STONE FOOTBRIDGE at the head of a fjord-like inlet. (The curious may now divert to Xlendi Tower on the point.) The sandy bay at **Xlendi** (**1h**), sheltering between sheer cliffs, must be one of the most visited spots on the island (Picnic 24a). Most visitors stop at one of the many bars and

restaurants for lunch or a drink. Walk into the car park at the rear of the waterfront buildings where the BUS STOP is located. Catch either BUS 306 OR 330 for the short journey of about two minutes to bus stop TUTA. (You could of course walk up the road, which will take about 15 minutes, but it is busy and there is no pavement.)
At the crossroads opposite the Tuta bus shelter turn left on a narrow road winding uphill through fields towards the ridge. You reach the hamlet of **Ta'Għajn Tuta** in just over five minutes (**1h05min**). Here turn left towards the sea on a narrow road (TRIQ GĦAJN TUTA), passing farms and enjoying wonderful

views towards the coast. Ignore all tracks left and right. On the outskirts of Kercem this road becomes TRIQ SARG (**1h20min**). Continue straight ahead until you reach the junction with TRIQ S PIETRU US PAWL, where you turn left, in two minutes reaching the centre of **Kercem** at PJAZZA SAN GRIGOR and the CHURCH.

Turn left here, passing more suburban housing. Then, in just over six minutes (**1h30min**), on the edge of **Santa Lucija**, fork left (where the right fork leads to the centre of the village). Open countryside beckons now as you follow this quiet road westwards along the RIDGE. At a fork (**1h40min**) keep left. A low

white communications mast stands some 250m/yds away to your right. At around **1h50min** you come to a little pond in the rock (the **Roman Lake**).

The walk bears right just past the pond. Five minutes later, at a downhill bend soon after passing between two quarries, turn right. Then, almost immediately, turn left (the fork to the right would take you into a quarry). One minute later, go left again at a cane windbreak, taking a narrow concrete-surfaced track down into a shallow *wied*. After crossing the *wied* the track climbs up through terraces. At one point the track has become blocked by stones that have fallen from

Xlendi — a very popular lunchtime destination for tourists

the adjacent embankment. It is necessary to divert left onto a path in the adjacent field which has been kept free of cultivation.

Beyond the obstruction, the path meets a footpath, where you head left to **Qawra Tower** (**2h35min**). The tower is open to visitors when the flag is flying, and the views from the roof are spectacular. Below is **Dwejra Bay**, which was once completely encircled by land. **Fungus Rock** (photograph page 26) is now all that remains of its outer rim. The rock was notable as the habitat of a rare fungus highly prized by the Knights for its medicinal properties.

From the tower make your way around to the tiny CHAPEL at **Dwejra** and thence to the **Inland Sea** between the chapel and the cliffs (**3h15min**). *Take note of warning signs on the seaward side of the Inland Sea and do not venture onto any part of the cliffs in windy weather.* This magnificent area takes on an almost mystical character when drenched in a fine sea-spray mist. The Inland Sea is an enormous collapsed cave, still with a tunnel to the open sea. Local fishermen provide boat

trips through the tunnel to view the high, almost vertical cliffs on the other side. To really appreciate the area, climb up past the chapel and walk round the rim of the crater.

It is possible to shorten the walk by catching bus 311 back to Victoria from Dwejra. For those keen on more walking, retrace your steps back past Qawra Tower. At the point where the footpath meets the track you climbed from the *wied* (**4h**), continue straight ahead on a narrow path, passing a QUARRY BUILDING. Ten minutes later, turn left at a track crossroads (beside a large house called L-GHABEX). A narrow BRIDGE takes you across the **Wied Ilma** and, in a few minutes, you bear right at a farmhouse, where a welcome SPRING feeds water into roadside troughs. On the hillside above are ancient caves which housed some of Gozo's earliest inhabitants.

A small road leads you into the pretty village of **Santa Lucija**. Bear right along TRIQ GHAJN GHABDUL, to reach PJAZZA SANTA LUCIJA, pass the market cross, and find your BUS STOP straight ahead in TRIQ BIR-RIX (**4h30min**).

See also photograph page 25
Distance: 7.1km/4.4mi; 2h
Grade: moderate; some scrambling between Mgarr and Mgarr ix-Xini. Ascent about 180m/600ft, descent 75m/250ft
Equipment: stout shoes, sunhat, swimwear, waterproofs, picnic, water
How to get there and return:
🚢 between Malta and Mgarr Harbour; if staying in Gozo, 🚌 301, 302 from Victoria to Mgarr; journey time 15min.
Short walk: Mgarr — Mgarr ix-Xini — Mgarr (4.3km/2.7mi to the tower; 1h15min; moderate, with an ascent of 140m/450ft and descent of 40m/125ft). Follow the main walk to Mgarr ix-Xini but, instead of crossing the bay, keep to its eastern side and follow the rough road up to

the former heliport and Santa Cilja Tower. Catch 🚌 301 to Victoria or Mgarr Harbour, or walk along the main road to the harbour. (It is also possible to use a parallel minor road on the right, just before the heliport (no passenger service); this leads into Triq Ta' Cordina in Ghajnsielem).
Alternative walk: Mgarr — Xewkija (6.7km/4.2mi; 2h; grade as Short walk 1). Follow the main walk to Mgarr ix-Xini. Cross to the western side of the bay and take the narrow road up the Wied Hanzira. Turn right through Xewkija and follow the map to the traffic lights on the north side of the village, where you can catch 🚌 301 to Victoria or Mgarr.

T he hustle and bustle of the ferry port of Mgarr are soon left behind as the walk heads westwards towards the highest cliffs in Gozo. The final stretch takes in the sprawling village of Sannat and the southern suburbs of Victoria.

Start the walk at **Mgarr harbour:** leave the harbour area and walk along the restored quayside past the GLENEAGLES BAR, then climb steps to reach SHORT STREET (**5min**). In less than 100m/yds, turn left at VELSON'S WINERY into TRIQ LOURDES. In a few minutes, near the top of the hill, rejoin the main MGARR/ VICTORIA ROAD near Fort Chambray, which has impressive walls and ditches. The fort dates from 1749 and was one of the last major projects during the rule of the Knights of St John. A housing development has recently been completed here. Proceed along the main road and in just under five minutes (**15min**) turn left

along TRIQ TA' CORDINA (there is a house called THE HAVEN at the junction). Your route follows some sleepy streets on the outskirts of the village of **Ghajnsielem**. First, in a few

Right: cliffs at Ta' Cenc

metres/yards bear right; then, a minute later, take a left turn onto a concrete track (TRIQ IX-XATT L-AHMAR) that leads downhill. Pass a small POND fringed by bamboo. Continue downhill; the track becomes rougher and deteriorates into a path within two minutes walking of a group of BOAT HOUSES (**25min**).

Turn right along the coastal track, passing saltpans and a splendid PRICKLY PEAR HEDGE (**30min**). Just past the hedge a minor road comes down from Ghajnsielem; there is parking and seats here, as well as a local INFORMATION BOARD. For those interested in military weaponry, there is a FOUGASSE on the foreshore that was used to discourage pirates. Your way becomes a footpath which runs parallel with the fields, on their seaward side. In just over **45min** you descend to a ROCK-CUT PLATFORM, where there are more SALTPANS (and a sewage outfall). After a prolonged spell of wet weather, it is likely that you will encounter a stream flowing over part of the rock-cut platform; *care* and some scrambling will be needed to get round this obstacle.

You will see your next landmark, the tower guarding the

entrance to **Mgarr ix-Xini** inlet;
it is reached in under **1h**. This
steep-sided valley was probably
the main port used by the
Knights of Malta (the name
means Harbour for Galleys)
and is a lovely swimming,
boating and fishing spot (Picnic
25).

It will take you fully 15 minutes
to reach the crossing point of
the *wied*. Once on the other
side, take the small road to the
right, pass the WATER TANK and,
50m/yds further on, at a passing
place on the road, turn left

*Right: Xewkija church seen
from near Ta' Cenc*

Mgarr ix-Xini

through a gap in the wall. Join a road that after three minutes acquires a tarmac surface and follow it south, winding through holiday bungalows. Fine views of the bay and tower should inspire you. At the bungalow TINA (**1h25min**), continue uphill on the road, ignoring a track on the left. There are views to Mgarr-ix-Xini and beyond to Comino, and soon the impressive church at Xewkija comes into view. The road borders an area of great archaeological interest, and on your left, a few minutes from the road, are the remains of **Borg Ta' L-Imramma**, a Copper Age temple.

A few minutes later, cart ruts of two different gauges can be found by taking a diversion just before reaching the boundary of

122

the HOTEL TA' CENC (**1h50min**). Turn left on a good track towards the cliffs and in four minutes, where it bears away to the left, continue straight ahead on a red-earth path until, after five minutes, the low wall on your right ends. Turn right and in 100m/yds come to short section of wall near the edge of the high vertical cliffs. Good examples of cart ruts can be found on the landward side of the wall. *This diversion adds 15min to the overall times. Great care is needed when approaching the cliffs in this area.*

Bear right around the hotel and ten minutes later you will be in the centre of the pristine village of **Sannat** (**2h**), where you catch the bus (Luqa stop) to Victoria.

Walk 26 GOZO: MGARR • HONDOQ IR-RUMMIEN • QALA • DAHLET QORROT • SAN BLAS BAY • IR-RAMLA • XAGHRA

See photographs on pages 14, 25, 33

Distance: 14.6km/9mi; 4h05min

Grade: moderate to difficult; overall ascent of about 520m/ 1700ft and descent of 460m/ 1500ft. Immediately after passing the marina there are some rock and clay slopes to negotiate. Some very rough terrain near Dahlet Qorrot. Beyond Dahlet Qorrot the walking is moderate, but sometimes steep.

Equipment: walking boots or stout shoes, sunhat, swimwear, waterproofs, picnic, water

How to get there: as Walk 23, page 111

To return: 🚌 307 to Victoria or 🚌 322 to Mgarr

Short walk: Mgarr — Qala — Mgarr (4km/2.5mi; 1h40min; moderate, with ascent/descent of 180m/600ft). Follow the main walk to the defensive wall (25min). Some 20m/yds before the eastern end of the wall,

climb up through a gap in the wall and take a path which leads to a track with a prickly pear hedge on the left and a wall on the right. After passing an abandoned building, bear right. Concrete comes under foot, and you meet a road coming down from Qala. Turn left here, to rise 60m/200ft to Qala. Turn left on Triq iz-Zew-wieqa (fine views to Comino and Mgarr harbour). Follow this road downhill, turning left in Mgarr to the harbour.

Alternative walk: Mgarr — Hondoq ir-Rummien — Qala — Nadur (7.5km/4.7mi; 2h; moderate, with an ascent of 230m/750ft and descent of 205m/675ft). Follow the main walk to the 1h20min-point. Instead of turning right towards the coast, bear left and then right, to reach the Nadur/Dahlet Qorrot road. Head left into the centre of Nadur, which is served by 🚌 302, 303, 322.

T his is the most arduous walk in the Gozo series. Like Walk 23, it takes in an area not visited by many tourists. On offer are rugged cliffs, two lovely coves and the best beach on the island.

The walk starts in **Mgarr**, at the GLENEAGLES BAR on the waterfront, where colourful fishing boats lie at anchor. Follow the road around the north side of the harbour, passing the MARINA. The road ends at a BREAKWATER (**10min**). Scramble through some rocks on the foreshore for a short distance, and then take the footpath leading to a DEFENSIVE WALL (**25min**) guarding a route inland. (*I would not recommend following the coastal path beyond this point: the ground slopes towards the cliff-edge, there is a risk of*

vertigo, and in a northwesterly wind this path is potentially very dangerous.)
Instead, about 20m/yds before the eastern end of the wall, climb up through a gap in the wall and take a path which leads to a track in about 100m/yds. A prickly pear hedge is some 20-30m/yds to the left, and there is an abandoned building on the right at about the **28min**-mark. Ignore the left turn; follow the right-hand fork towards the sea. In about five minutes (**33min**) this track briefly acquires a concrete

surface, and in another minute it meets a road. *(The Short walk goes left here.)* Turn right and, at about the **40min**-mark, the road ends at a farm building. Just before it ends, turn right on a path heading downhill towards the coast, then follow the coastal path round to **Hondoq ir-Rummien** (**55min**; Picnic 26a).

Climb the access road out of the bay, past the MADONNA TAL-BLAT chapel (from its belvedere there are fine views of Comino and the Blue Lagoon visited on Walk 27. In ten minutes you reach a small CHURCH and the QALA PARISH CEMETERY (**1h05min**) on the left, on the outskirts of Qala. Turn immediately right uphill into TRIQ SANTA MARIJA TAL-

QALA. In two minutes, at a FARM, turn right by a SEAT and a small GARDEN. Three minutes later, where there is a right turn into a QUARRY, turn left towards Qala. You come upon one of Gozo's classic landscapes — fields in the foreground, and church spires and the Qala windmill on the horizon.

Follow the road into **Qala**. Bear right into a narrow street (TRIQ TA'SEMPER; **1h17min**). Then turn right into TRIQ IL-MITHNA; a house at this junction is dated USA 1983 and has sunflower decorations on its balconies. (A short detour to the left would take you to the privately-owned windmill.) At a crossroads reached in little more than one minute, continue straight ahead into TRIQ TA'GULJU. Four minutes later the track descends steeply. Soon you meet a fork: go right (the Alternative walk goes left here).

Descend gradually to a small WATCHTOWER (**1h40min**). Continue towards the coast and turn left on the coastal path. After ten minutes some steps take you down to **Dahlet Qorrot** (**1h55min**; Picnic 26b), a colourful bay with boat houses built into the cliff. Carry on around the bay, taking the minor road up the western side. At **2h**, 50m/yds past some prickly pears, follow a track to the right, just below the cliff, and make your way around the hill. After about ten minutes

(**2h15min**), come to a TANK at the foot of the cliff and cross over a PIPE, bearing left uphill. The footpath leads into a track, passing a FARM, and emerges on a ROAD (**2h30min**).

Turn left and, on the outskirts of **Nadur**, take the first right (opposite a FARMHOUSE WITH A PLAQUE AND SHRINE on its front wall).* Then bear right again at VILLA SAN BLAS. Just after passing a small garden (**2h35min**; Picnic 26c) the road takes you down into **San Blas Bay** (**2h45min**; Picnic 26d). Just before the bottom of the road, take the left-hand fork, passing cane wind-breaks sheltering citrus groves.**

From the beach (very popular with the local people) proceed initially up the watercourse of the **San Blas Valley**, passing the fishermen's huts. Then cross the stream and bear right uphill, through a pretty patchwork of gardens where, at the right season, oranges and lemons ripen in the shelter of rubble walls and cane windbreaks. After climbing for about ten minutes, come to a TRACK at the base of the cliff on the west side of the valley (**3h**). Follow this for five minutes, then turn right on asphalt and in a few minutes go straight ahead (ignoring the right turn which is the OLD RAMLA BAY ROAD).

In another three minutes (**3h10min**) you meet a wide, recently upgraded road at a

---

*In wet weather, the climb out of San Blas Bay is very slippery; take this alternative route. Instead of turning right at Villa San Blas, go straight ahead for a minute, to a viewpoint with seats. Descend to the valley on a very narrow road and reach a crossroads where Triq Wied Bingemma comes down the valley on your left. Continue

straight ahead, climbing steadily. At about the 9min-mark, turn right, and in a further three minutes join the main walk at the junction with the old Ramla Bay road (12min). Pick up the main walk just before the 2h30min-point. This reduces overall walking time by approximately 20min.

T-junction where there is a large CEMETERY on the left. BUS STOP Qasab is on the left here (Buses 302, 322) if you wish to shorten the walk. Otherwise turn right downhill (there is a pavement) and in 10 minutes, at the foot of the hill (**3h20min**) pass BUS STOP Ramla. Turn right again, to **Ramla Bay** (**3h25min**). This is one of the largest sandy beaches in the Maltese Islands, but it can be an exposed spot when the wind is from a north or north-westerly direction.

From the bay retrace your steps up the main valley road. Ignore the first road to the right, but in a further 200m/yds, take the *next* right turn (where the main road that you walked down earlier swings left uphill towards Nadur (**3h30min**).

Continue past a series of DAMS and turn left on a track (where the road begins to climb towards Xaghra; **3h55min**). Ignore a left turn in about one minute, and after passing a HORSE FARM ignore the right turn (by some rusty gates). But in a further minute, *do* turn right uphill on a track. A small stone building is off to the left just past this junction. Pass a POND on the left and, some 100m/yds up the track, a telegraph pole on the

right. The track winds through small fields, and near the top it twists to the left and exits on a road on the outskirts of **Xaghra** (TRIQ IT-TAFLA; **4h20min**).

The route to the NEOLITHIC TEMPLES OF GGANTIJA involves turning right towards the centre of Xaghra. Continue straight on in one minute (at the next junction) into TRIQ PARISOT, and go left in a further three minutes into TRIQ JOHN OTTO BAYER, where you pass the VILLA PORTELLI, an impressive house built in the style often adopted by returning emigrants who have spent their working lives in Australia, Canada or the United States. Two minutes later, turn left again (TRIQ L-IMQADES).

The entrance to **Ggantija** is on the left at this point, while the **Ta' Kola Windmill** is visible on your right a short distance away along TRIQ IL-MITHNA. A combined ticket can be purchased for both historic sites, while the museum shop is only two minutes walking along TRIQ L-IMQADES — where you can catch a bus at the Templiji BUS STOP for Victoria or Marsalforn (**4h30min**). The BUS STOP (Bayer) for Mgarr is adjacent to the Villa Portelli.

**An optional detour offers the opportunity to explore local agriculture and traditional irrigation techniques in the small rock gardens close to the Mistra Rocks which lie between San Blas Bay and Dahlet Qorrot. Just before the bottom of the road, where the main walk forks left, bear right. Follow the road to its end at a turning point (5min). Follow the higher track (ignoring any paths to lower plots on your left) to an irrigation tank overlooked by a large boulder. Ahead lie the fear-

some Mistra Rocks, huge boulders interspersed with thorny bushes. Return to the turning point. The left-hand path, on slightly lower ground, leads to another irrigation tank at the edge of the cultivated area. *From here a faintly defined path leads into the rocks, but don't be tempted to explore one of the least-visited parts of the islands — there are crevasses, dangerous crumbling, man-made walls and the risk of losing your way.* Allow *an extra* 20min for the higher route and 35min for both routes.

See also photographs pages 7, 9
Distance: 8km/5mi; 2h05min
Grade: easy, with an overall
ascent/descent of 190m/620ft
Equipment: stout shoes, sunhat,
swimwear, waterproofs, water
How to get there and return:
🚢 Comino Ferries Co-op Ltd
run a scheduled service to the
Blue Lagoon from Marfa (near
the Riviera Hotel) and
Cirkewwa (adjacent kiosk on
the quayside). The company
also run timetabled services
from the Blue Lagoon to Mgarr,
Gozo. There are fewer sailings
in winter — and the service may
be cancelled in poor weather.
Do check sailing times and
weather conditions before
travelling to Marfa or Cirkewwa
(see pages 132-133 for details).
Short walk (4.8km/3mi;
1h10min; easy, with an overall

ascent/descent of 100m/340ft).
Follow the main walk to Santa
Marija Bay. Retrace your steps,
passing the deserted cottages
and, 50m/yds further on, turn
right and follow a wide track
downhill past the entrance to
the Comino Hotel (there is a
building with a blue door here).
Another five minutes' walking
will see you back at the Blue
Lagoon.
Alternative walk (8.6km/5.3mi;
2h10min; easy, with an overall
ascent/descent of 190m/620ft).
*This walk is intended for those
staying at the Comino Hotel.*
Follow the track uphill out of
the hotel grounds and turn right
to reach the Blue Lagoon. Then
follow the main walk until it
completes the circuit of Comino
before coming to the start of the
track leading back to the hotel.

C omino is the third island in the archipelago and has
a unique atmosphere ... few residents and hardly any
vehicles! It is the ideal place to go on a fine Sunday, when
Malta's roads are choked with traffic, and huge queues at
the ferry terminals frustrate travel to and from Gozo. The
island derives its name from cumin, a herb similar to
fennel. Peace and quiet prevail here, helped by the
island's status as a bird sanctuary.

Since it is most convenient to
arrive aboard the Comino Co-op
ferry, the walk starts at the
SLIPWAY at the **Blue Lagoon**
(Picnic 27; photograph page 9).
Its iridescent green- and blue-
hued waters are sheltered by the
small island known as Comi-
notto. In high season a fleet of
yachts and cruise boats from
Malta will be anchored here,
but happily part of the lagoon is
roped off for the exclusive use of
swimmers. This has become a
very popular spot, and there is a
toilet/shower block and mobile
vans supply refreshments to
visitors. However, for much of

the year only the arrival of the
passenger ferry briefly disturbs
the peace, and you will need to
bring your own supply of food
and drinks.
Start out by walking along the
coastal path in the direction of
Comino Tower, keeping well
away from the overhanging cliff-
edges and any inlets in the cliffs.
This is a spectacular setting: the
indigo sea, brooding sea cliffs
and the offshore islets, with the
distant cliffs of Gozo as a
backdrop are perfect for photography. Continue on around
two small bays, and at **25min**
the path turns up right to

Comino Tower (built in 1618). Unfortunately the tower is not open, and the walkway around the tower at entrance door level is roped off for safety reasons as there is no fencing.

The old ISOLATION HOSPITAL, built in the 1890s to aid the recuperation of British servicemen returning from plague-affected ports in the Levant, is your next port of call. The track now runs north, and the curious may wish to divert to the OLD CEMETERY on the hill; otherwise, continue straight ahead — and note the wide track to the left about

50m/yds before some DESERTED COTTAGES grouped in a compound: this track will be your route towards the end of the walk.

In just under five minutes (**40min**) come to a tiny CHURCH (where services are still held), surrounded by trees. The POLICE STATION, which is above a little boathouse, is your next target, reached two minutes later. Carry on to the 'South Sea Island' Beach, **Santa Marija**, fringed with tamarisk trees and vitex shrubs. Walk along the beach, then cut inland on a

Comino Tower

track leading uphill just beyond the public CAMPING SITE (some 80m/yds before a jetty). You pass **Comino Major**, rising to just 75m/247ft on the left. The next landmark on this section of the walk are the extensive but disused buildings of the PIG FARM, which was built to restock Maltese farms after the 1980 swine-fever epidemic. Turn right here and, almost immediately, turn left on a narrower track, keeping the buildings of the pig farm on your left. Past here the track drops steeply towards the South Comino Channel with views to northern Malta, where the hotels strung out along the

shoreline are a striking feature. Turn left to visit the restored **Santa Marija Battery** which was built in 1715. You can explore the interior and the ramparts, provided the access gate is open (**1h10min**).

Leaving the battery, continue along the coast on a good track which runs about 30m/100ft above the gently-sloping south coast of the island. In **1h30min** come to a turning down to **Smugglers Creek**, in which according to local legend lies the wreck of a small ship laden with contraband cigarettes. Soon you are back at **Comino Tower**. Retrace your steps past the ISOLATION HOSPITAL to the wide track junction before the DESERTED COTTAGES (**1h50min**). Turn left and follow the track which gradually descends past a patchwork of walled and cane-edged fields to **San Niklaw Bay** — a pretty, but private beach belonging to the Comino Hotel. Go straight ahead past the entrance track to the hotel, near a building with a BLUE DOOR (**2h**). In another five minutes you reach the **Blue Lagoon** (**2h05min**), for the return ferry.

The old Isolation Hospital

BUS AND FERRY INFORMATION

MALTA

Malta Public Transport operates a scheduled bus service throughout Malta and Gozo. The latest timetable information is given on their website publictransport. com.mt (tel: 2122 2000). This includes summary timetables for every route; an expanded timetable with details of every bus stop served on each route, a travel planner, and updates of changes/disruptions to services. Below I list selected services to and from the walks and picnics in this book, as well as handy routes serving the resorts. This information is more easily understood if it is read in conjunction with the Bus Route Map which can be downloaded from the website or obtained at bus termini and tourist offices in Malta and Gozo.

Bus Services from VALLETTA

Destination	Route	Average frequency	Last bus from destination
Bahar ic-Caghaq	13	30min	22.45
Birzebbuga	82	20min	22.55
Bugibba	31/45/48	10min	22.40*
Buskett Gardens (via Dingli)	56	hourly	19.45
Cirkewwa (for Gozo and Comino ferries)	41/42	15min	21.55**
Cospicua (Bormla)/	4	30min	22.45
Vittoriosa (Birgu)	2	10min	23.08
Dingli	52	30min	22.30
Ghadira Bay	49	hourly	21.17
Ghajn Tuffieha/ Golden Bay/Mgarr	44	30min	21.30
Gharghur	46	30min	21.35
Marsascala	91/93	15-30min	22.55
Marsaxlokk	81	20min	22.55
Mosta (served by buses to Bugibba and Cirkewwa)			
Mtarfa	51	30min	22.35
Pembroke	14	30min	22.40
Qrendi	72	30min	22.30
Rabat/Mdina	51/52/53	10-20min	22.41***
Senglea (Isla)/ Cospicua (Bormla)	1	20-30min	22.25
Siggiewi	62	20-30min	22.16
Sliema Ferry (also served by routes 13 and 14)	15	30min	22.30
Vittoriosa (Birgu)	2	20min	22.05
Xghajra	94	20min§	23.12

*Bus 31; **Bus 41; ***Bus 51; §Bus 94 hourly after 19.10

Selected express and direct bus services in Malta

X1: Airport/Marsa Park & Ride/Mater Dei Hospital/Bahar ic-Caghaq/Mellieha/ Cirkewwa: every 45 minutes
Last bus departs Cirkewwa 22.30

X3: Airport/Marsa Park & Ride/Rabat/Mosta/Bugibba: hourly
Last bus departs Airport 22.30, Bugibba 22.15

101: Mgarr/Golden Bay/Manikata/Mellieha/Cirkewwa: hourly
Last bus departs Mgarr 20.50, Cirkewwa 21.00

103: Bidnija/Pembroke Park & Ride: hourly
Last bus departs Bidnija 19.15 and terminates at Naxxar

109: Bahrija/Santi/Rabat/Zebbug/Siggiewi/Providenza (Bajjada bus stop): hourly
Last bus departs Bahrija 20.45, Bajjada 21.45

124: Senglea (Isla)/Marsacala: hourly
Last bus departs Marsascala 21.30

181: Dingli/Buskett Gardens/Rabat/Mater Dei Hospital: hourly
Last bus departs Dingli 20.15, Buskett 20.17

201: Rabat/Siggiewi/Hagar Qim/Blue Grotto/Zurrieq/Airport: hourly
Last bus departs Rabat 20.42, Airport 20.45

202: Sliema Ferry/Rabat: hourly
Last bus departs Rabat 22.00

221: Bugibba/Mellieha/Cirkewwa: 30-60 minutes
Last bus departs Cirkewwa 21.50

222: Sliema Ferry/Mellieha/Cirkewwa: 30-60 minutes
Last bus departs Cirkewwa 21.55

223: Golden Bay/Bugibba: hourly
Last bus departs Golden Bay 21.00

225: Golden Bay/Sliema Ferry: hourly
Last bus departs Golden Bay 20.55

GOZO

The walks in this book have been written up for easy access from Malta. Two of the walks begin at Mgarr harbour; the other two start from Victoria, after a short journey on the 301 bus from Mgarr. A timetable for all Gozo bus services can be obtained from the Tourist Information Office in Victoria. The times listed below are for the winter schedule (November to mid-June).

Bus services from Victoria, Marsalforn and Mgarr harbour

301: Victoria/Xewkija/Mgarr 05.30-23.00: every 25-45min
Last bus departs Mgarr 23.25

302: Victoria/Nadur/Ramla 08.05-19.05 (earlier and later services terminate at Nadur): hourly
Last bus departs Ramla 19.33

303: Victoria/Nadur/Qala/Mgarr 05.00-22.45: every 45-60min
Last bus departs Mgarr 22.30

305: Victoria/Ta' Cenc (Sannat)/Munxar/Victoria 05.05-22.35: every 45-60min
Last bus departs Ta' Cenc 22.46

306: Victoria/Xlendi 05.05-22.48: hourly
Last bus departs Xlendi 23.00

307: Victoria/Xaghra 06.05-22.05: hourly
Last bus departs Xaghra 22.33

308: Victoria/Ghasri 05.00-21.55: hourly
Last bus departs Ghasri 22.00

309: Victoria/Zebbug 05.00-22.25: hourly
Last bus departs Zebbug 22.39

310: Victoria/Marsalforn 05.30-23.30: hourly
Last bus departs Marsalforn 22.50

311: Victoria/San Lawrenz/Dwejra 07.20-19.20: hourly
Last bus departs Dwejra 19.38

Bus at Qrendi church

Emergency telephone numbers

EU-wide emergency telephone number: 112 (operators answer only in Maltese and English)

Ambulance 196

Police: 2122 4001-7

Traffic accident: 2132 0202

Fire brigade: 112

Patrol boat rescue: 2123 8797, 2122 5040

312: Victoria/Gharb/San Lawrenz 05.00-23.02: hourly
Last bus departs Gharb 23.17
313: Victoria/Santa Lucija/Kercem 05.00-21.37: hourly
Last bus departs Santa Lucija 21.48, Kercem 21.50
322: Marsalforn/Zebbug/Nadur/Mgarr 05.10-21.40: hourly
Last bus departs Mgarr 22.25
323: Victoria/Xewkija/Ghajnsielem/Mgarr 05.20-22.20: hourly
Last bus departs Mgarr 22.45
330: Victoria/Fontana/Xlendi 09.05-17.05: every 2 hours
Last bus departs Xlendi 17.18

Malta-Gozo ferry service
This service is operated by roll-on/roll-off vehicle ferries belonging to the Gozo Channel Company, Channel House, Mgarr Harbour, Mgarr, Gozo GSM2480 (www.gozochannel.com; tel: 2210 9000; e-mail: admin@gozochannel.com). The trip from Cirkewwa at the northern tip of Malta to Mgarr harbour takes about 25 minutes. Sailings operate at 45 minute intervals between 05.45 (Malta departures) and 06.00 (Gozo departures) until 21.45 and at a frequency of approximately 1h30min at other times.

Comino ferry service
Comino Ferries Co-op Ltd: www.cominoferries.com; tel: 9983 5766/9940 6529/9967 4112; e-mail info@cominoferries.com.

Winter schedule
Departs Cirkewwa (adjacent kiosk on quayside): 10.00, 11.00, 12.00, 13.00, 14.00, 15.00
Departs Blue Lagoon, Comino, for Malta: 10.30, 11.30, 12.30, 13.30, 14.30, 15.30
Departs Blue Lagoon, Comino, for Gozo: 12.15, 14.15

Please note that there are earlier and later trips in the summer months, and that this service also departs from Marfa harbour (opposite the Riviera Hotel)

Index

Geographical names comprise the only entries in this index. For other entries, see Contents, page 3. Maltese place names (see page 31) follow the better-known English names which have been used in the text. Some place names *not* used in the text are also included. A page number in *italic type* indicates a map reference; a page number in **bold type** indicates a photograph. Either of these may be in addition to a text reference on the same page. (M) = Malta, (G) = Gozo, (C) = Comino. See also Bus and Ferry timetables, beginning on page 131.